Graphis Mission Statement: Graphis is commited to presenting exceptional work in international design, advertising, illustration and photography. Since 1944 we have presented individuals and companies in the visual communications industry who have consistently demonstrated excellence and determination in overcoming economic, cultural and creative hurdles to produce brilliance.

DesignAnnual2003

The International Annual of Design and Illustration
Das internationale Jahrbuch über Design und Illustration
Le répertoire internationale du design et de l'illustration

CEO & Creative Director: B. Martin Pedersen

Editor: Michael Porciello

Art Director: Lauren Slutsky
Design & Production: Nicole Recchia, Luis Diaz,
Alexia Leitich, and Joanne Sullivan

Published by Graphis Inc.

This book is dedicated to
Ikko Tanaka
(1930-2002)

(opposite) Corporate Identity for Power One (detail) by Haefelinger Wagner Design, p. 85

Made By Package Land

http://www.package-land.com

Contents Inhalt Sommaire

Remarks: We extend our heartfelt thanks to contributors throughout the world who have made it possible to publish a wide and international spectrum of the best work in this field. Entry instructions for all Graphis Books may be requested from: **Graphis Inc.**, 307 Fifth Avenue, Tenth Floor, New York, NY 10016, or visit our Web site at www.graphis.com. *Anmerkungen:* Unser Dank gilt den Einsendern aus aller Welt, die es uns ermöglicht haben, ein breites, internationales Spektrum der besten Arbeiten zu veröffentlichen. Teilnahmebedingungen für die Graphis-Bücher sind erhältlich bei: **Graphis Inc.**, 307 Fifth Avenue, Tenth Floor, New York, NY 10016. Besuchen Sie uns im World Wide Web, www.graphis.com. *Remerciements:* Nous remercions les participants du monde entier qui ont rendu possible la publication de cet ouvrage offrant un panorama complet des meilleurs travaux. Les modalités d'inscription peuvent être obtenues auprès de: **Graphis Inc.**, 307 Fifth Avenue, Tenth Floor, New York, NY 10016. Rendez-nous visite sur notre site web: www.graphis.com. © Copyright under universal copyright convention copyright © 2002 by Graphis Inc., 307 Fifth Avenue, Tenth Floor, New York, NY 10016. Jacket and book design copyright © 2002 by Graphis, Inc. No part of this book may be reproduced in any form without written permission of the publisher. ISBN: 1-931241-13-9 Printed in Hong Kong. Distributed in North America by Publishers Group West. Distributed in all other countries by HBI/HarperCollins.

(opposite) Self-promotional Shopping Bag by Package Land Co., Ltd., p.239

歌舞伎の発見

誰でもわかる歌舞伎の見方

富田鉄之助　著　白金書房刊

助六由縁江戸桜　勧進帳　鳴神　矢の根　毛抜　解脱　不破
暫　不動　象引　寿曽我　対面　菅原伝授手習鑑　神霊矢口渡
国性爺合戦　蘆屋道満大内鑑　嫗山姥　小野道風青柳硯
仮名手本忠臣蔵　平家女護島　傾城反魂香　義経千本桜
博多小女郎浪枕　源平布引滝　一谷嫩軍記　壇浦兜軍記
奥州安達原　鬼一法眼三略巻　八陣守護城　忍夜恋曲者
御所桜堀川夜討　祇園祭礼信仰記　加賀見山旧錦絵
本朝廿四孝　鎌倉三代記　妹背山婦女庭訓　絵本太功記
敵討天下茶屋聚　伊賀越道中双六　近江源氏先陣館
恋女房染分手綱　摂州合邦辻　伽羅先代萩　楼門五三桐
曾根崎心中　近頃河原の達引　桂川連理柵　艶容女舞衣
天竺徳兵衛韓噺　東海道四谷怪談　双蝶々曲輪日記
女殺油地獄　大経師昔暦　恋飛脚大和往来　新版歌祭文
生写朝顔話　心中天網島　伊達娘恋緋鹿子　積恋雪関扉
夏祭浪花鑑　伊勢音頭恋寝刃　廓文章　お染の七役　茨木
京鹿子娘道成寺　連獅子　草摺引　素襖落　土蜘蛛　紅葉狩
春興鏡獅子　六歌仙容彩　船弁慶　舌出三番叟　釣女藤娘
与話情浮名横櫛　彩間苅豆　乗合船　恵方万歳　三社祭
四千両小判梅葉　水天宮利生深川　十六夜清心　吉原雀
籠釣瓶花街酔醒　神明裏和合取組　五大力恋緘　手習子
人情咄文七元結　怪異談牡丹燈籠　佐倉義民伝　鳥羽絵
蔦紅葉宇都谷峠　東海道中膝栗毛　明烏花濡衣　神田祭
天衣紛上野初花　梅雨小袖昔八丈　大岡政談　黒塚
盲長屋梅加賀鳶　巷談宵宮雨　元禄忠臣蔵　名月八幡祭
刺青奇偶　桐一葉　番町皿屋敷　一本刀土俵入　双面水照月
沓手鳥孤城落月　鳥辺山心中　修禅寺物語　暗闇の丑松

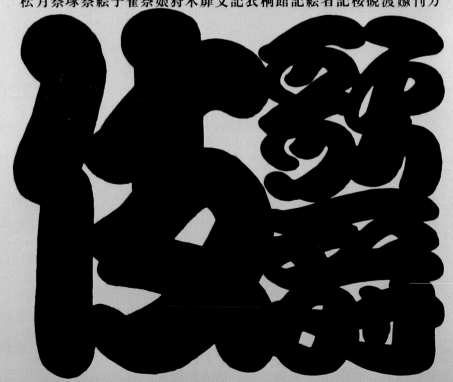

IKKO TANAKA
(1930-2002)

Master graphic designer Ikko Tanaka passed away on the 10th of January, 2002, at the age of 71. In hopes that designers active today will take to heart the lessons Tanaka taught in his work, it is to his memory that we dedicate this volume. Study the world, investigate the truths of your surroundings, and believe in the power of design. Tanaka was born in 1930 in Japan's ancient capital, the southwestern city of Nara. A childhood spent there—where the scent of antiquity lingered too strongly, thought Tanaka as a young man—nonetheless endowed him with a special connection to the aesthetic traditions of his country. By the time he was working, Tanaka was superbly prepared and unequivocally determined to translate the essence of intricate traditional subjects into graphics for the modernizing world of postwar Japan. At the same time, he embraced the incredible economic transi-

graphic designer in a burgeoning market; throughout his life, Tanaka educated himself, and his audience, through his work. His choices for subjects were never simple ones—among his graphic yield were books, calendars and posters explaining The Rice Cycle: The Grain that Created a Culture; Wabi, Sabi, Suki: The Essence of Japanese Design; Sankei Kenze Noh; The Wheel: A Japanese History; Japanese Design—Tradition and Modernity; Japanese Color; Japanese Style; and Man and Writing.

Ikko Tanaka studied the world because it excited him. He delighted in discovering the essence of his subjects, unearthing his own reactions, memories and emotions, and conceiving of an entirely appropriate form for each message. The result was always both publicly effective and an expression that could not be separated from the man who created it.

tion of Japan, and with his work helped propel the populace into a new frame of mind and a new way of life, one that encompassed both tradition and innovations never imagined.

Ikko Tanaka's professional life, beginning just five years after the end of World War II, followed a trajectory of dramatic scale. Within a few years of graduating from the Kyoto College of Art, at the age of 24, he had won the prestigious Mainichi Newspaper's Industrial Design Prize. The next half century was his: He was intimately involved in every national and design event, from the founding of the Nippon Design Center and the hosting of the World Design Conference to the design of the comprehensive graphics of the Tokyo Olympics and the Osaka Expo. Every assignment he undertook seemed to be chosen for its cultural depth and importance to the redefinition of a ravaged nation.

With his creative direction of the young, dynamic Seibu retailing group, Tanaka defined the 1970s and 1980s. And yet he consistently approached subjects greater than the necessary commercial fare of a

Tanaka learned his methods of introspection and expression from the traditions of Tea and Noh theater, in which abbreviation is more powerful than augmentation, and clarity is paramount. He studied Tea until the end of his life, and was fascinated by the way it honed his appreciation of beauty in the slightest details.

Tanaka's visual expression—posters, typography, book design or art direction—was powerful because he had fire in his soul; Ikko Tanaka believed that design mattered. Near the end of his life, he worried aloud that design had become "too much of an occupation," he said, "just a trade." Taking Art Nouveau posters as an example of perfection, Tanaka mused that their beauty lay in their entanglement with their purpose and the age itself. A poster should tell the story of the times, he said, and a hundred years later the viewer should be able to nearly taste the period, in all its vitality. Ikko Tanaka's legacy is this belief.

With this Design Annual, we salute his memory. — Maggie Hohle

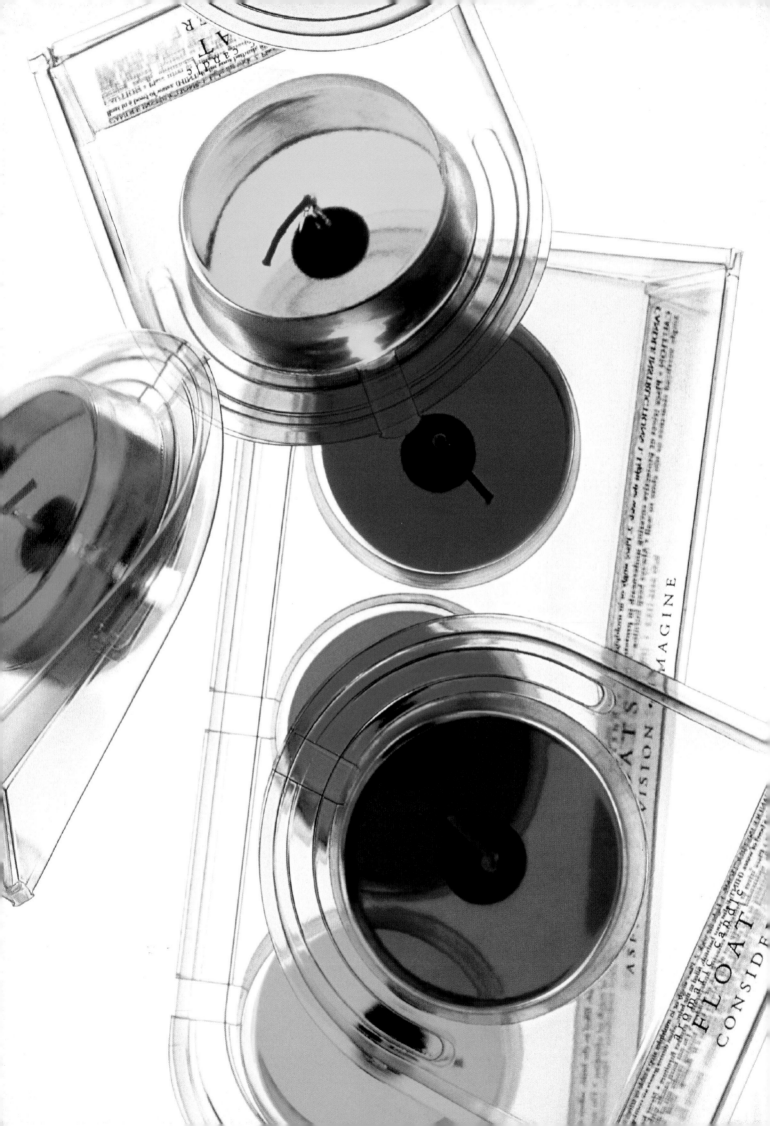

20 Questions on Design by Veronique Vienne

20 Questions on Design by Veronique Vienne

What is your proudest achievement in design so far?
I guess I haven't had it yet. Even though I try my best on each project, each time, "proudest" is hardest to achieve.

How much of your workday is spent on actual design?
Quite a lot in a day, actually. Including midnight!

Do you think that having a distinctive style is important?
In a way, yes. Occasionally clients come to you because you have a style. However, we have to be careful not to produce the "same trick" for every client's project.

How do you keep up with current trends in design?
They (the trends) are everywhere. You have to have the guts to not be a slave to them.

How much does technology influence your work?
A lot. The way you work, the materials you use...

What part of your work do you find most demanding?
Coming up with ideas, and realizing them within a time and budget!

Has globalization changed the way you work?
The internet really helps me work with overseas clients.

Have you ever turned down a client—and why?
I have. Most of time it's because of our schedules, sometimes it's simply the wrong match.

What questions do your clients most often ask?
I ask them the questions.

Where would you like to be ten years from now?
Tokyo or NY? I really don't know.

Which of your skills would you most like to perfect?
All of them!

How do you see your work evolving in the next five years?
Again, I really don't know...

How important is it to win awards?
It's lucky to have them.

How involved are you with the design community?
I love what I do.

Do you enjoy speaking at design conferences?
I would if I could speak better.

Name the three designers you most admire.
I have more than three designers to admire.

Do you teach a course on design?
No.

Do you have a philosophy on design that you would like to pass on to students?
The 3 Cs: Courage, Confidence and Continue.

What interests do you have outside work?
Going to Onsen! (Japanese style Spa & Hot Spring) and hanging out with friends.

Over to you—any final words on design?
It's tough, but it's fun!

Tokyo native Sayuri Shoji studied design at the School of Visual Arts in New York. After freelance experience with Kiyoshi Kanai Inc., Calvin Klein Inc. and Eiko Ishioka, Inc., she established "Sayuri Studio, Inc." in New York City. The studio was recently moved to Tokyo, where she continues to develop work for an international roster of clients. Her work has been recognized by the New York Art Directors Club, Communication Arts, the AIGA, ID Magazine and the Tokyo Art Directors Club.

(opposite, and previous page) Packaging designs by Sayuri Studio for Sephora and Issey Mikake, Inc.

BEWARE WET PAINT

Beware Wet Paint Designs by Alan Fletcher presents graphic design from the hands and thoughts of a contemporary master. These are demonstrated with 250 examples of work produced for major clients around the world, or just for his own amusement. Grouped into thematic chapters, the examples show his concepts and references, his lithe and lateral jumps, his ability to fuse interpretation, aesthetics and function with apparent ease. Personal observations and four essays give further critical and biographical insight into the work, and the man. Each of the designs is accompanied with a commentary by **Jeremy Myerson**.

PHAIDON

What is your proudest
achievement in design
so far?
*Still being asked to
do a job.*

How much of your
workday is
spent on actual design?
About 48 hours a day.

Do you think that
having a distinctive style
is important?
Probably.

How do you keep up with
current trends in design?
Engage.

How much does
technology influence
your work?
Not too much.

What part of your work do
you find most demanding?
Invoicing.

Has globalization changed
the way you work?
Silly question.

Have you ever turned
down a client—and why?
Yes. They were too boring.

What questions do your
clients most often ask?
Where do you get ideas?

Where would you like to
be ten years from now?
Where I am now.

Which of your skills would
you most like to perfect?
*Making a long distance
phonecall on the first try.*

How do you see your
work evolving in the next
five years?
Unravelling.

How important is it to
win awards?
*Depends on who's giving
the award.*

How involved are you with
the design community?
Quite a bit.

Do you enjoy speaking at
design conferences?
Half yes, half no.

Name the three designers
you most admire.
*Many, but here are three:
Thomasweski, Andre
Massin,
Pierre Fauchaux*

Do you teach a course
on design? *No.*

Do you have a philosophy
on design that you
would like to pass on
to students?
No—I don't have one.

What interests do you
have outside work?
None.

Over to you—any final
words on design?
None.

*Alan Fletcher belongs
to that élite
international group of
designers who have
transcended the
conventional boundaries
of their craft.
He helped form the now
legendary design
consultancy Fletcher
Forbes Gill, and was a
founder member of the
design group
Pentagram. He has
tackled every facet of
design with a unique
style and purpose.
No one else inhabits
the world of ideas,
of wit and ambiguity in
graphic design in
quite the same way. Alan
Fletcher has come to be
depicted as that
less-is-more,form-follows-
function dogma and
somehow found a
way to, well, relax.
He is currently
consultant Art Director
to Phaidon Press.*

*(opposite)*Beware Wet
Paint; Designs By Alan
Fletcher—*One of the many
extraordinary book cover
solutions that Alan has exe-
cuted for Phaidon Press.*

Q/A with Steve Sandstrom

What is your proudest achievement in design so far?
I think it is the firm that my partner Rick and I have created. The quality of the people, their talents, commitment and intelligence is substantial. I know that at any moment something great can happen at the studio. It is a nice place to work and play. The work, I think, speaks for itself.

How much of your workday is spent on actual design?
My workday is 9.5 to 14.5 hours long. I include thinking as part of design, so my estimate is that a low would be 65 percent and a high would be 90 percent.

Do you think that having a distinctive style is important?
Having a distinctive style can be the quickest way to become recognized in design. Of course, that style must be appealing enough to generate success. And I believe that most designers develop an overall sense of personal style that is more evident when reviewing the sum of their work, than it is from project to project. I feel that developing a distinctive style is important for a designer. Most clients do not receive the full benefit of work done for them when it looks just like work done by the designer for several other clients. The designer's signature is on all, but where's the client's signature? To me, it is more exciting to develop a style for the client. Every client becomes a new opportunity to exercise your creative skills. It would be a boring, self-centered life for me to channel every client through my own narrowly developed, distinctive style machine.

How do you keep up with current trends in design?
Mostly observation, and a little instinct developed over experience. I try to be open-minded. I read and review and try to take in as much as I can when I travel. I'm interested in all areas of design; architecture, product and industrial design, advertising, fashion, etc.

How much does technology influence your work?
The Mac has enabled me to explore more complicated executions with less concern about the labor-intensive nature of such concepts or about degree of difficulty. Technology has put typography in my control and responsibility. (That's good and bad.) When technology saves me time, it only creates more demanding deadlines and the necessity to do even more work in less time. It also provides a visual language of digits and pixels. Opens up lines of communication and allows for more long distance client relationships.

What part of your work do you find most demanding?
Problem solving and thinking—trying to execute at a level that I feel excited about.

Has globalization changed the way you work?
Globalization has allowed for us a diverse clientele. At times international. But the way we work really hasn't changed. We've had Swedish clients, and needed to learn some differences between that culture and ours. Which is still the most difficult thing to overcome. What is funny to an American, may not be to a Swede. What is cool to an Austrian may not be to an American.

Have you ever turned down a client—and why?
We have a relatively small studio of around 15 people. At times we have been too busy to take on more work and have had to turn it down. We try to do work for clients that we fit well with. It is not our goal to grow the firm, so we want to be doing work that is fun and challenging and an opportunity for us to do a great job. That doesn't mean that we handpick every project and not every project is a perfect assignment. We just try to be somewhat careful about the work we take on and the kind of clients we establish relationships with. We probably turn away 25 percent of the requests that come our way.

What questions do your clients most often ask?
Clients always want to know costs and timing, especially if they don't already have that pre-determined. They want to know who will be working on their materials and what their responsibilities are. They want to know who their key contact is. They want to know about our "process" and how we would approach working with them.

Where would you like to be ten years from now?
Ten years from now, I would like to experience the same quest for good ideas and thrill of executing them for great clients. I would like to have as much enthusiasm about the studio and our staff as I have today. So much can happen in ten years. I will probably have to deal with a partnership transition by then. Hopefully, that would be a thoughtful, successful, and good transition.

Which of your skills would you most like to perfect?
I do not want to perfect any skill. That in itself seems flawed. People are not perfect and there should always be room for improvement.

How do you see your work evolving in the next five years?
The next five years will probably be a steady climb out of a down economy. It will take awhile for budgets to grow back. A more robust economy breeds new companies. And I think we are very capable at developing identities and personalities, packaging, etc. for new business ventures. What we can't guarantee, of course, is their complete success. But we typically get them off to great starts and help create more potential opportunities. So I feel we will have more work for start ups and I hope we are able to continue developing many of our existing relationships.

How important is it to win awards?
We use awards and publication as a new business tool. In that way, it is important. It can also help recruit personnel whenever there is an opening on staff. Our awareness and reputation have been built in large by our exposure through award shows and annuals.

How involved are you with the design community?
I am not overtly involved in the local design community. I do represent that business by being on the board of the Portland Ad Federation and by helping to expand design into that organization. I also judge many shows, both ad and design and have presented design winners for the One Show and the Clio Awards. These are ad-oriented organizations that I have helped consult with and have offered insights about the design business. I try whenever possible to educate organizations and companies outside of our business about design. I feel I can help the design community as a whole by championing beyond ourselves.

Do you enjoy speaking at design conferences?
I haven't spoken at any of the large design conferences. I have presented to marketing organizations, colleges and educational, local and regional design and advertising chapters around the country. I enjoy meeting new people and if I do anything that inspires someone, that's great. I am mostly very honored to be asked to speak. That is a validation that people are interested in our work and what we have contributed to the industry.

Name the three designers you most admire.
Not sure I could narrow it down to three. I am always more impressed with designers outside of graphics like Frank Gehry and Philippe Staark, Armani, Miyake. It's easy to say Paul Rand. I think I admire his intelligence more than his art. I don't know how to get it to three. There are too many I admire and even more that I should.

Do you teach a course on design?
No.

Do you have a philosophy on design that you would like to pass on to students?
For everything you learn about design, try at the very least to learn as much about something—anything—else.

What interests do you have outside work?
(no comment)

Over to you-any final words on design?
(no comment)

In 1989, Steve Sandstrom joined forces with Rick Brathwaite to set up Sandstrom Design. The Portland native's branding work for clients ESPN, Hollywood Video, Tazo Teas and the Miller Brewing Company has earned him widespread recognition. His work was profiled in Graphis Issue 326.

(opposite) Sandstrom Design's packaging for Tazo Teas includes a built-in infuser for brewing anywhere.

(this spread) Design Firm: VSA Partners, Inc. Creative Directors: Dana Arnett and Ken Fox Designer: Jason Jones Photographer: Charlie Simokaitis Copywriters: Jack Sichterman and Reid Armbruster Client: Harley-Davidson

THE
RIDE
GREAT RIVER ROAD

Sunday 3:26 PM

Not yet ... no, not yet. Your body tells you it's not quite time to upshift into third. It doesn't feel right. It's not time. A millisecond later the world aligns; a synchronized motion of hand and foot will result in a seamless increase in power to the rear wheel. For a Harley rider, that is a defining moment, when operator and machine are one. Your fingers tense, your foot rises slightly. But your instinct and experience tells you it's not time; not yet ... no, not yet.

EXPERIENCEBUSINESS
Harley-Davidson, Inc. 2000 Annual Report

THE
LIFESTYLE
BATON ROUGE, LOUISIANA

Monday 7:12 AM

You back your motorcycle into a spot out front and lean it on the sidestand, satisfied with the miles you just left behind. The parking lot is almost empty, but soon it will be filled with dozens of Harley™ motorcycles, each as unique as its owner. Each with its own story to tell. You dismount and take off your helmet, gloves and jacket, anticipating a well-deserved cup of coffee and a chance to catch up with friends. But your ride doesn't end here. In fact, you're just getting started.

FINANCIAL OVERVIEW

Numbers are revealing, but they hardly begin to tell the story of why Harley-Davidson is successful. Ask our customers about return on investment and they'll show you some pictures they took in the Badlands. Talk to our dealers about the bottom line and they'll send you on a ride with their local H.O.G.™ or B.R.A.G.™ chapter. They understand what you're asking, but for them, it's not just about selling motorcycles. It's about making experiences. It's about making memories of a lifetime.

25

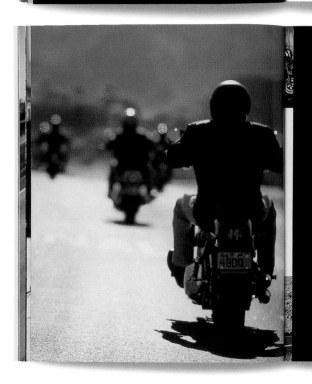

THE
CONNECTION
CODY, WYOMING

Thursday 12:53 PM

After several miles of serene straightaway, the "curves ahead" road sign is a welcome sight to everyone. The ride is about to change dramatically. Instinctively, we increase the distance between bikes and lean forward in our saddles, focusing on the road ahead. Ten bikes weave through a series of turns. Ten throttles react with precision. Ten heart rates quicken, as if controlled from the same network. Not a word is spoken. But we understand each other perfectly.

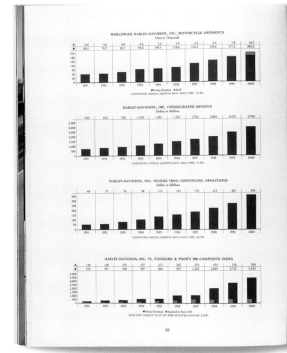

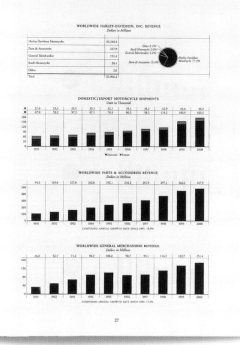

26

27

ENTRY: ....

✳✳✳✳✳✳✳✳✳✳✳✳✳✳✳✳✳✳
McKNIGHT — 2000
THE POWER OF SYNERGY
✳✳✳✳✳✳✳✳✳✳✳✳✳✳✳✳✳✳

ENTRY: ....

Contents

www.mcknight.org

THE McKNIGHT FOUNDATION
ANNUAL REPORT 2000

ENTRY: ....

Fig. 1

{ "THOUSANDS OF LETTERS AND CALLS FROM A WIDE VARIETY OF
ORGANIZATIONS AND INDIVIDUALS HAVE A DRAMATICALLY GREATER CHANCE OF INFLUENCING PUBLIC
POLICY THAN CONTACTS GENERATED FROM ANY SINGLE ORGANIZATION."
DAN CRAMER, GRASSROOTS SOLUTIONS, CONSULTANT FOR THE ALLIANCE OF EARLY CHILDHOOD PROFESSIONALS

ENTRY: ....

Organizing

NO. 1

CASE STUDY	SPECIFICS
READY-4-K CAMPAIGN	STATEWIDE GRASSROOTS ORGANIZING TO REFORM EARLY CHILDHOOD POLICIES

The challenge? Unifying thousands of early childhood professionals and organizations into a force compelling enough to drive system and policy reform from the bottom up. Right now, in different ways and settings, they all work passionately on many of the same issues. But to achieve a scale of change that ensures children's well-being across the state, they must lay aside competing agendas and values and speak to policymakers with one voice.

The answer is grassroots organizing: the old-fashioned, messy, hands-on, absolutely powerful bedrock of democracy. Ultimately, large, diverse groups of determined people have the best chance of successfully carrying strategies for change up the policy ladder, of translating public will into better education and better care for young children.

There are no short cuts to the sprawling, ground-up, coalition-building process of citizen action, but it yields a crucial by-product— new leaders. Those who were passive become active; those who saw the bare outline of the problem become highly informed, politically astute organizers; those who thought they had no say discover their right to be heard. While empowering others, they empower themselves.

What does the Ready-4-K campaign hope to achieve? Nothing less than the reform of policies drafted when the world of childhood was a completely different place, and the redesign of a system made obsolete by radical gains in knowledge. Nothing less than every child in Minnesota being fully prepared for success in kindergarten and the rest of their school careers.

How are they going to do it? Together. By building a network of networks. By marrying grassroots organizing to social marketing. By educating and inspiring not only members of their own profession, but citizens in all walks of life to create an unstoppable state movement on behalf of young children.

2000 GRANTEE
THE ALLIANCE OF EARLY CHILDHOOD PROFESSIONALS
$150,000 OVER THREE YEARS

A Hybrid Market

Once upon a time, not so very long ago, the words "retail trade" conjured up an image of a general store selling a variety of basic commodities directly to families and individuals. This image has changed over time: into large department stores, and then huge suburban malls, chain stores and franchises, as the growth of a post-industrial mass market transformed the Retail Industry during the 1900s. As we approached the end of the 20th century, an even greater catalyst for change, the Internet, revolutionised and irreversibly transformed the way commodities and services are sold and distributed to the general public.

Not everyone believes that the Internet is destined to take over as the primary channel of retail commerce; but no retailer can ignore its importance. All retailers must adapt to the new economy in order to survive. And as the scenario becomes ever more complex, both global and local players are confronting new and often unpredictable challenges in meeting the needs of a large volume of diverse customers who vary widely in their requirements, preferences and behaviour.

Trends and challenges in the Retail Industry

- The advent of the Internet and other technology requires that retailers are able to sell goods and interact with customers through a variety of channels of communications
- Entrance barriers for new players have decreased, dramatically heightening competition and putting pressure on ever-decreasing margins
- Customer power has grown, and retailers must respond to high expectations from increasingly demanding consumers
- Defection barriers for customers are low, and loyalty is more difficult to secure and keep
- Transaction volumes over the Internet are growing rapidly, placing pressure on customer tracking, billing and related services

In the hybrid Internet/over-the-counter mass marketplace, retailers must find new and innovative ways to interact efficiently with a large number of customers, responding to their individual needs and fulfilling their expectations. But, as margins are pressed downwards, all retailers must find ways to differentiate themselves from their competitors in the eyes of the demanding customer. To do this, they must be able to use all their assets, one of the most valuable of which is the information they gain about their customers and their preferences.

2000 Annual Report

Welcome to a New Age
of Customer Management Solutions

c.Rel

---

c.Rel's solution for the Petroleum Retail Industry

c.Rel's unique CRM solution, c.Rel Enterprise, was specially developed to fulfil the complex needs of the Petroleum Retail Industry. It is a comprehensive, fully integrated system, and offers these unique advantages to the Petroleum Retail Industry:

Flexible marketing database   Petroleum retailers, with their often well-established payment card schemes, need to both process transactions and organise and use the information gained from the transactions. c.Rel Enterprise incorporates a marketing database that enables retailers to capture large amounts of data from various internal and external sources through easily adaptable interfaces, and then to organise the information in one customer-centric data structure. All relevant data, such as demographics, preferences and buying patterns, can be used in segmentation for targeted communication and tailored reward programs. c.Rel Enterprise's string campaign management tool provides automated and efficient marketing capabilities.

Reward and loyalty programmes   Reward and loyalty programmes have become essential marketing tools in all retail industries. With one of the most sophisticated reward management systems in the market, c.Rel Enterprise enables petroleum retailers to reward customers through bonus systems and offer value-added incentives and benefits to the most loyal and profitable customers.

Integrated card management   c.Rel Enterprise is the only truly integrated fuel/bank/pre-payment/loyalty card-processing system in the marketplace. The c.Rel Enterprise application fully supports partner and third-party card schemes, providing both merchant settlement and clearing functions. c.Rel Enterprise's functionality will greatly simplify migrations and linkages over less-integrated software applications that maintain separate databases for individual card schemes. This allows for easy migration of existing customers to new card schemes (either fuel or loyalty) and the capability to consolidate and add new card schemes. Card schemes supported include:

- Membership/loyalty
- Pre-payment
- Consumer revolving
- Consumer charge
- Corporate fleet
- Corporate truck
- International truck
- Real-time

With increased Internet usage, the capability to process, validate, and authorise data in a real-time mode will become essential for leading petroleum retailers. c.Rel Enterprise is a true real-time system in which transactions – both fuel card and loyalty – are immediately and directly posted, giving accurate and up-to-date information about the customer and merchant.

'X Factor' Design Firm: Equus Design Consultants P/L Art Directors: Andrew Thomas and Alex Mucha Designers: Chung Chi Ying and Gan Mong Teng Illustrator: Michael Lui Copywriter: Andrew Thomas Client: Craft Print International

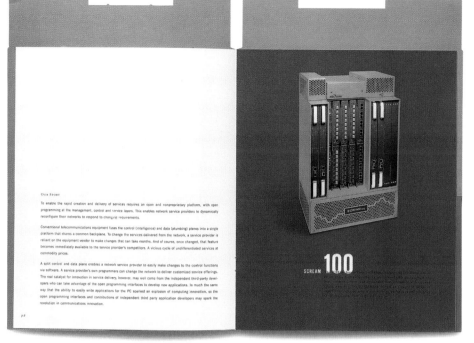

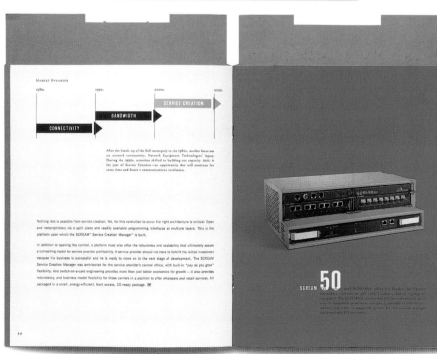

Client: Network Equipment Technologies, Inc.

Annual Reports 20,21

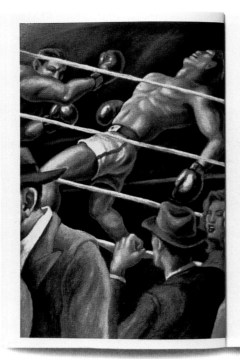

CHAPTER 1

REPORTS OF OUR
DEMISE

IN MARKETS WE ONCE LED
(OR SHOULD HAVE)—HIGH-END STORAGE,
UNIX SERVERS AND DATABASE
SOFTWARE—WE'RE BATTLING BACK
AND MAKING UP LOST GROUND.

PAGE NO.
THIRTEEN

YOU'RE ONE PAGE AWAY
from the NO-HOLDS-BARRED STORY
of ONE YEAR
in THE LIFE OF A COMPANY.

It's the story of
BIG BATTLES,
STINGING DEFEATS
&
GRITTY COMEBACKS.

UNEXPECTED ALLIANCES,
DARING FORAYS
&
GAME-CHANGING
DISCOVERIES.

In many ways,
IT'S A STORY ABOUT THE FUTURE,
AS WELL AS THE RECENT PAST,
AND ABOUT ALL BUSINESS TODAY.
WHICH MEANS IT'S ABOUT E-BUSINESS.
AND ONE IN PARTICULAR.

IBM
ANNUAL REPORT 2000

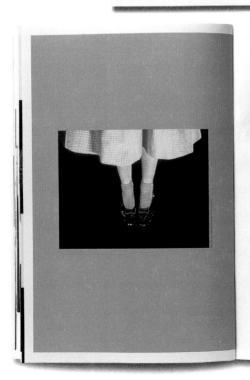

CHAPTER 5

COMING
HOME

HOW THE WORLD'S LARGEST PROPONENT
OF E-BUSINESS IS TRANSFORMING
ITS PROCESSES AND CULTURE TO BECOME
THE WORLD'S LARGEST E-BUSINESS.
AND SO IT BEGINS.

When does a business become an e-business? Until recently, the answer seemed to be: when you can buy something over its Web site. Today, we know better. It's when you work with your customers, take and *fulfill* orders, provide services, procure billions of dollars in goods and services, interlock with your suppliers—and support thousands of employees in scores of countries around the world to learn, collaborate and work in real time...on the Web. That's how we're helping our customers become e-businesses. And it all starts at home.

PAGE NO.
FORTY-ONE

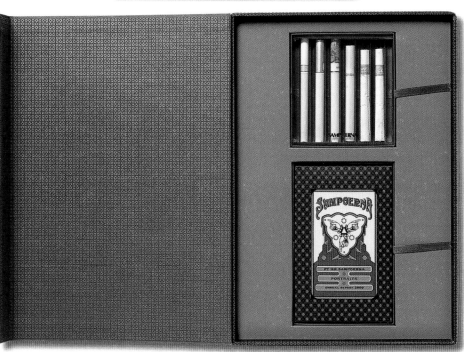

Design Firm: Epigram Creative Director: Edmund Wee Art Director: Wong Wai Han Designer: Wong Wai Han Photographer: Frank Pinckers Copywriter: Jonathan Zax Client: Pt Hm Sampoekna Tbk.

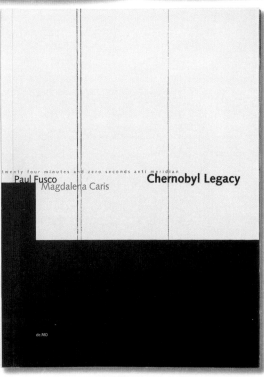

twenty four minutes and zero seconds anti meridian

Paul Fusco
Magdalena Caris

Chernobyl Legacy

de.MO

(this spread) 'Chernobyl Legacy' Design Firm: de.MO Creative Director: Giorgio Baravalle Photographers: Paul Fusco and Magdalena Caris

The institution is situated approximately 10 kilometers from Minsk, Belarus

Novinki 216
Children's Mental Asylum

stories about 216 children aged

At birth most of these children are so horrifying a revelation to their parents that they are immediately abandoned to the state. They are left mostly to themselves. Some play with other children, but many cannot even move without help. Many live solitary lives reacting in secret with the phantoms that inhabit them.

When the children of Novinki come of age they will be transferred to the main insane asylum to live out the rest of their lives their future a mystery.

Dr. Natasha Yegorava who has been treating radiation victims since 1986 said:
There is no way out. Very often there is no way we can help some people.
Our Children are not healthy now. They all have weakened immune systems and genetic damage .... my country is dying.

Pages 124,125 DIMA "mamma... mamma... mamma" Mother is no longer visiting Dima, 16 years old.

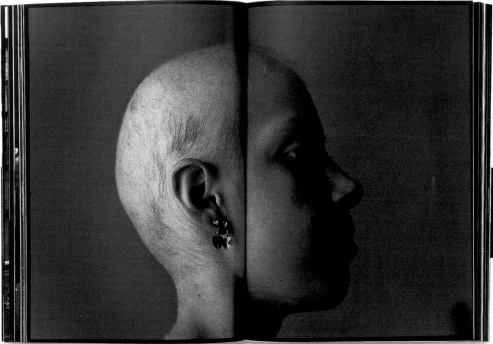

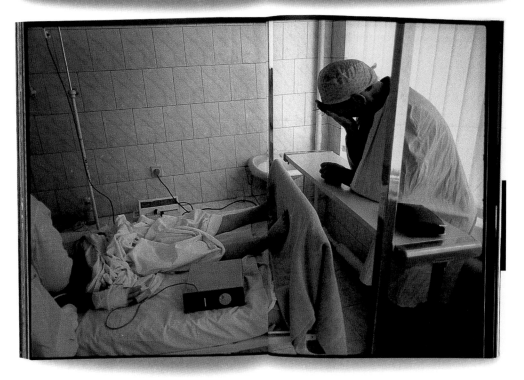

ANIMAL
LONGINGS

The
STILL LIFES
of
KATE BREAKEY

A. D. COLEMAN

Bombycilla cedrorum
CEDAR WAXWING
1991

Coccyzus americanus
YELLOW-BILLED CUCKOO
1 9 9 8

Coccyzus erythropthalmus, Yellow-billed Cuckoo

Passerina cyanea
INDIGO BUNTING I
1 9 9 7

Helianthus annuus
SUNFLOWER
1 9 9 8

Falco sparverius, American Kestrel (Sparrow Hawk)

Falco sparverius
AMERICAN KESTREL
1 9 9 8

Hasan Türkmen

Kiler

Şiirler

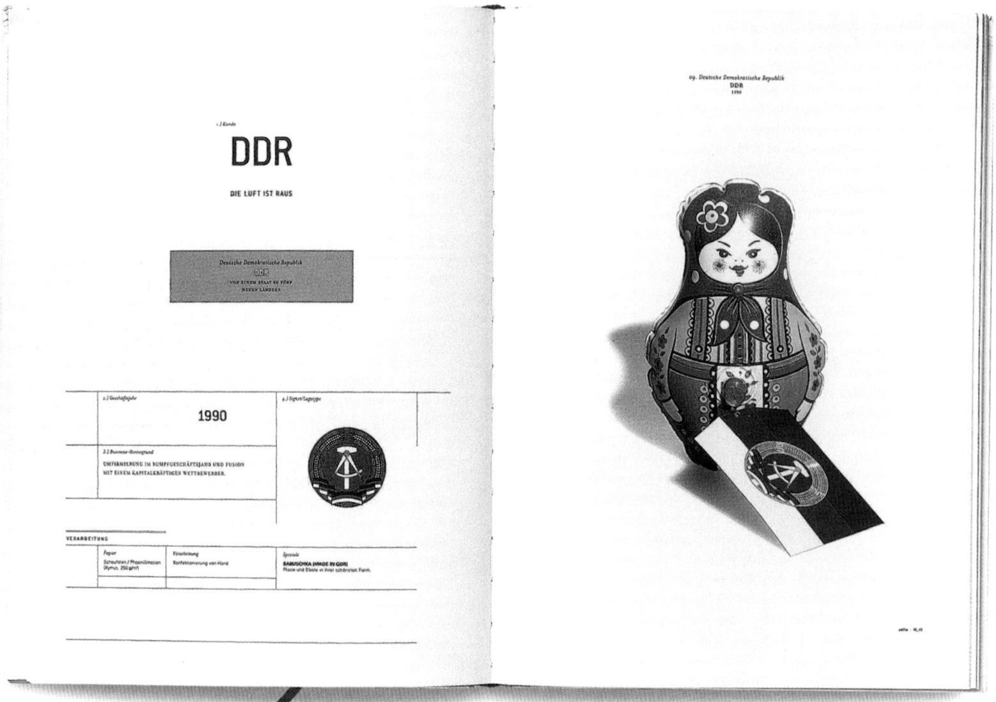

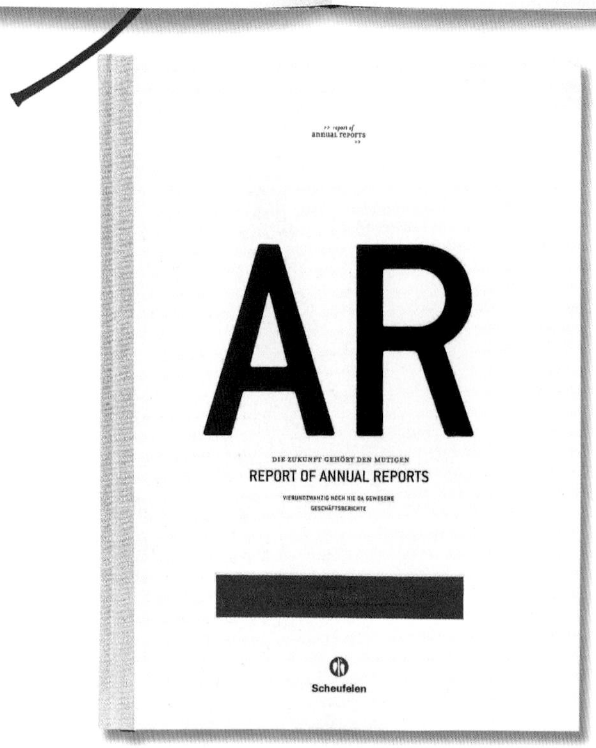

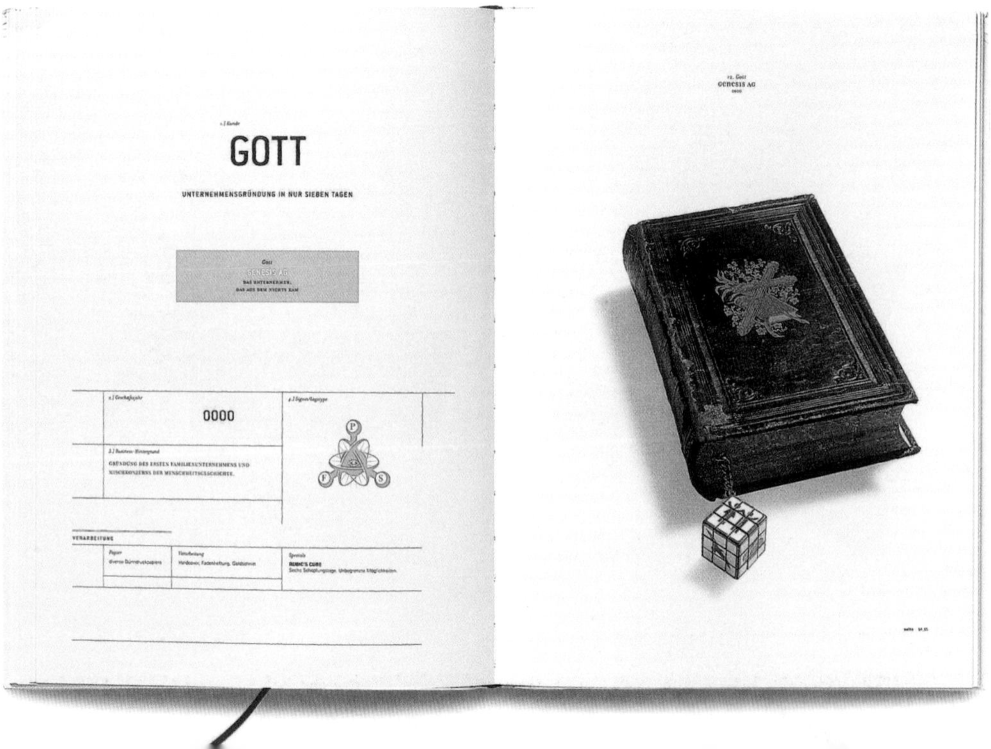

(this spread) 'Report of Annual Profits' Design Firm: Strichpunkt GmbH Creative Directors: Jochen Rädeker and Kirsten Dietz Art Directors: Jochen Rädeker and Kirsten Dietz Designers: Caroline Abele, Katja Deml, Kirsten Dietz, Tanja Günther, Felix Widmaier, Jochen Rädeker and Stephanie Zehender Photographers: Andreas Langen and Kai Loges Illustrators: Gernot Walter and Felix Widmaier Copywriters: Karl Böhm and Jochen Rädeker Client: Papierfabrik Scheufelen

GEBRÜDER GRIMM

FAKTEN STATT FIKTIONEN

	1854	

LOUIS BRAILLE

BRINGT DIE SCHRIFT AUF DEN PUNKT

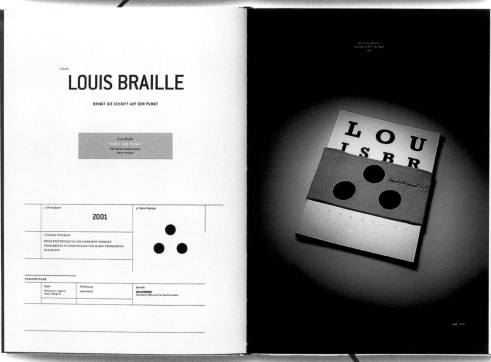

	2001	

DIE MAFIA

VERBRECHEN ZAHLT SICH AUS

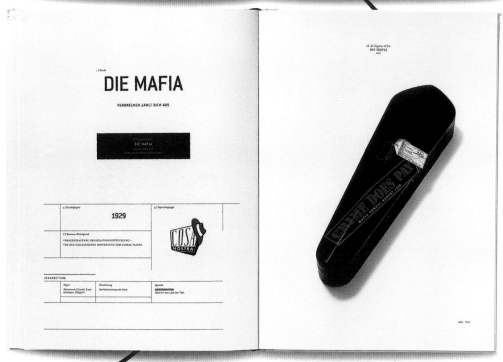

	1929	

(this spread) 'Typography 22' Design Firm: Gail Anderson Art Director: Gail Anderson Designers: Gail Anderson and Ken DeLago Photographer: Bob Grant Client: Type Directors Club

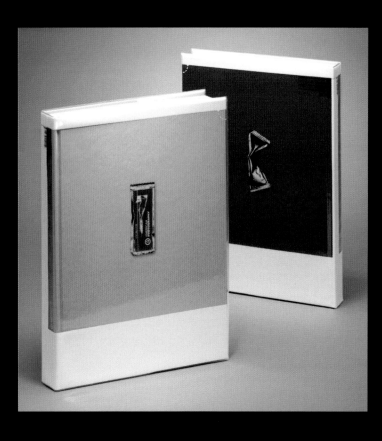

American Photography' Design Firm: 344 Design, LLC Creative Director: Stefan G. Bucher Designer: Stefan G. Bucher Photographer: Craig Cutler Copywriter: Peggy Roalf Producers: Mark Heflin and Gary Koepke Client: AImIus, Inc.

John Berryman
77 Dream Songs

Wallace Stevens
Harmonium

Wendy Cope
Making Cocoa for Kingsley Amis

Seamus Heaney
North

Ted Hughes
New Selected Poems
1957–1994

Seamus Heaney
Station Island

Philip Larkin
Collected Poems

Michael Hofmann
Acrimony

Ted Hughes
Crow
From the Life and Songs of the Crow

Seamus Heaney
Sweeney Astray

Simon Armitage
Selected Poems

T. S. Eliot
Four Quartets

James Joyce
Poems
and shorter writings

Paul Muldoon
Quoof

Ezra Pound
Personæ
Collected Shorter Poems

Robert Lowell
Life Studies

Mark Ford
Soft Sift

Philip Larkin
The Whitsun Weddings

Louis MacNeice
The Burning Perch

Christopher Reid
Katerina Brac

Douglas Dunn
Elegies

Derek Walcott
Tiepolo's Hound

Seamus Heaney
Field Work

Thom Gunn
The Sense of Movement

Tom Paulin
Fivemiletown

'Poetry Series' Design Firm: Pentagram Design, Ltd. Art Director: Justus Oehler Design Assistant: Matthew Richardson Client: Faber & Faber

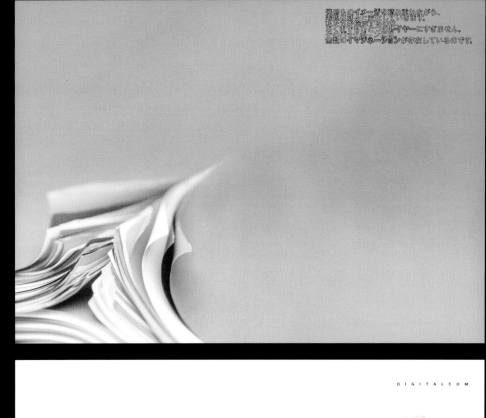

観客をのイメージを喚起させながら。
...
...イヤーにすぎません。
無限のイマジネーションが存在しているのです。

 DIGITALCOM

株式会社デジタルコム
〒107-0061 東京都港区北青山 3-10-6 青山パークス3F Phone:03-3409-3255 Fax:03-5466-7709 www.digitalcom.co.jp

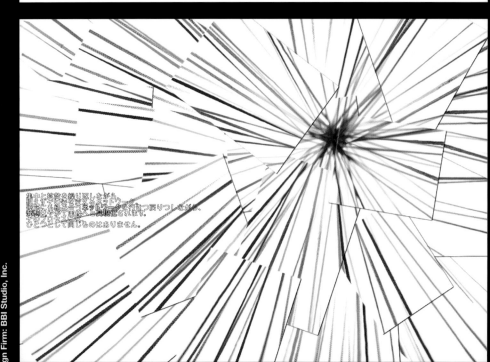

集中と放散を繰り返しながら。
...ネットワーク社会...
...電...
ひとつとして同じものはありません。

パワーは、関節の差分によって生み出されます。
流れとキックサイクルによって伝わる。
筋肉とパワーの差分。
間とはじる熱のエネルギーが波り出されます。

Sentra SE-R Spec V shown in Lava Orange with optional equipment.

速

六速王°

オメガドライブ

日産パフォーマンスを秘めて
スーパーエナジーレーサー
今、ここに誕生。

SE
R

01 SPORT BUCKET SEATS

02 RED-LIT GAUGES

03 6-SPEED MANUAL

'2002 SE-R Cards' Design Firm: The Designory, Inc. Creative Director: C. Fukunaga Art Directors: Siew lin Cheah and Eng Tang Copywriter: John Beck Client: Nissan North America

(this spread) '2002 G-Class' Design Firm: The Designory, Inc. Creative Director: Ulrich Lange Art Director: Matt Coonrod Photographers: Steve Cooper and Michael Rausch Copywriters: Kevin Helms and Felipe Bascope Client: Mercedes-Benz USA

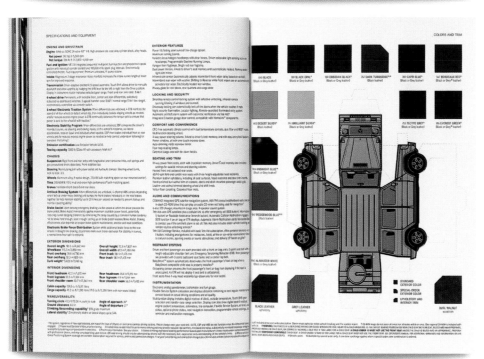

'Book of Be' Design Firm: Peterson & Company Creative Director: Miler Hung Art Director: Miler Hung Designer: Miler Hung Photographer: Lee Emmert Copywriters: Tiffany Hewson, Kevin Hope, Miler Hung and Nathan Coughey Make-up Artist: Tiffany Hewson Client:

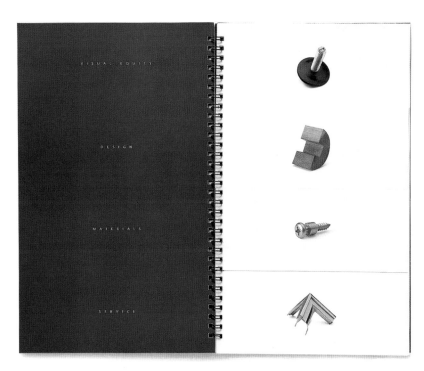

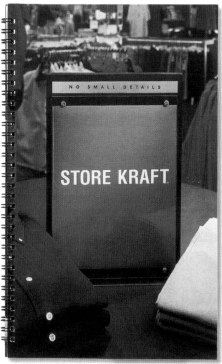

'No Small Details' Design Firm: Bailey Lauerman Creative Director: Sean Faden Art Directors: Ron Sack and Scott Loftus Photographer: Bob Ervin Copywriter: Nick Main Client: Store Kraft

Delphine Hirasuna Client: Potlatch Paper Co.

One of the industry's most rigorous corporate design competitions, the Potlatch Annual Report Show is widely regarded as the premiere annual report event of the year. The 2001 competition attracted more than 655 entries. Out of this group, our distinguished panel of judges singled out 26 books that met its criteria for design excellence and originality. Additionally, winners were singled out for the best in editorial development and print production. Congratulations to the winners and all those who have labored to elevate the art of annual reports.

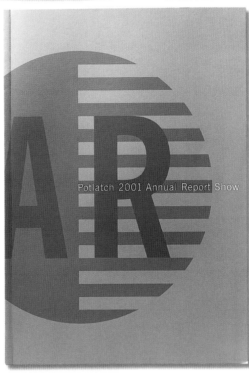

Potlatch 2001 Annual Report Show

(this spread) 'Potlatch 2001 AR Show' Design Firm: Pentagram Design Inc. Art Director: Kit Hinrichs Designer: Belle How Photographers: Barry Robinson, Marc Norbert and Tom Tracy Illustrators: Barbara Banthien, Justin Carroll, Will Nelson and Colleen Quinn Copywriter:

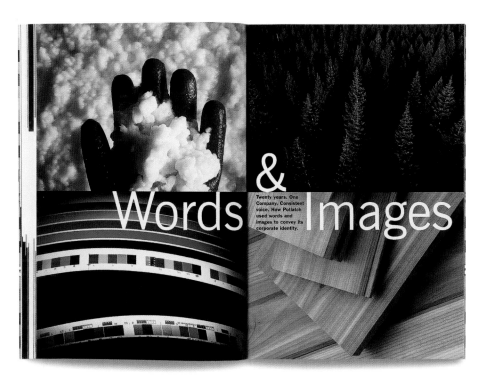

Words &Images

Twenty years. One Company. Consistent voice. How Potlatch used words and images to convey its corporate identity.

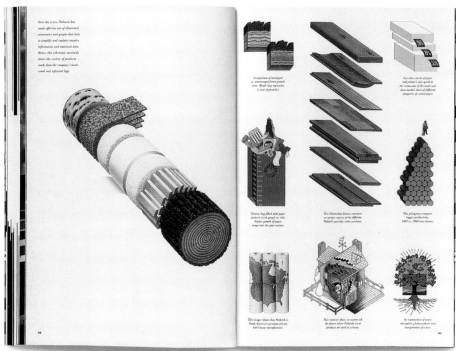

A sense of modern technology is communicated through long shots and intense close ups, documentary scenes and abstract images.

'Performance Place Brochure' Design Firm: Graphica Design & Communications Creative Director: Mark Stockstill Art Director: Cindy Schnell Designer: Susan Dorenkemper Client: Second & Main

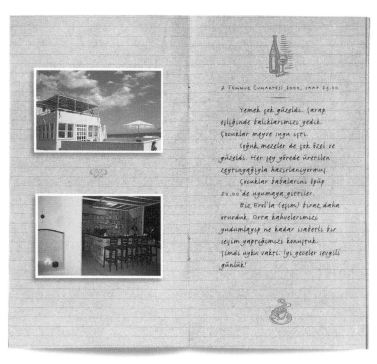

'Bir Yaz Hatirasi' Design Firm: Savas Cekic Design Studio Creative Director: Savas Cekic Art Director: Savas Cekic Designer: Savas Cekic Photographer: Kerim Yanik Copywriter: Turgay Kanturk Client: EGE Motel

'Annie Kuan Alu' Design Firm: Sagmeister, Inc. Art Director: Stefan Sagmeister Designer: Stefan Sagmeister Client: Anni Kuan Design

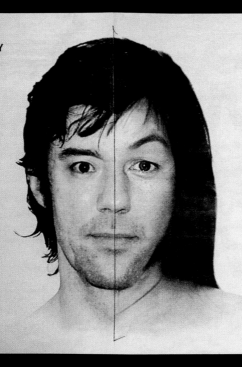

ANNI KUAN HAPPILY
INVITES YOU TO THE
FASHION COTERIE
IN NEW YORK CITY

TO PREVIEW THE
SPRING/SUMMER
COLLECTION 2002

FROM SUNDAY **SEP. 23**
TO TUESDAY **SEP. 25 2001**
BACK AT PIER 92

REPRESENTED BY

CYNTHIA OCONNOR + COMPANY
141 WEST 36 STREET, SUITE 12A
NEW YORK, NY 10018

TEL 212 594 4999
FAX 212 594 0770

ANNI KUAN DESIGN
242 WEST 38 STREET, 11 FLOOR
NEW YORK, NY 10018
TEL 212 704 4038
FAX 212 704 0651

ANNI KUAN

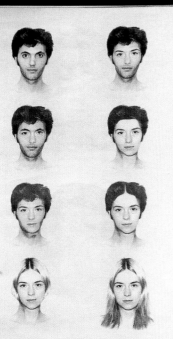

TANK TOP IN WATERMELON MATTE JERSEY WITH CHIFFON RUFFLES

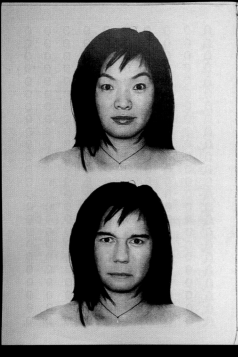

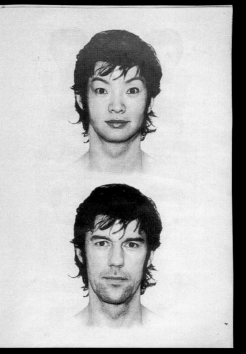

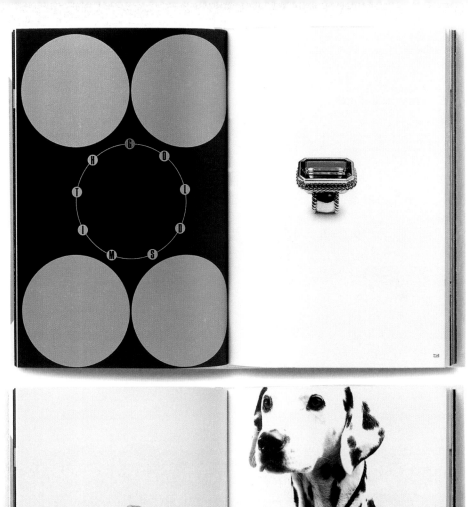

monday to saturday

sunday

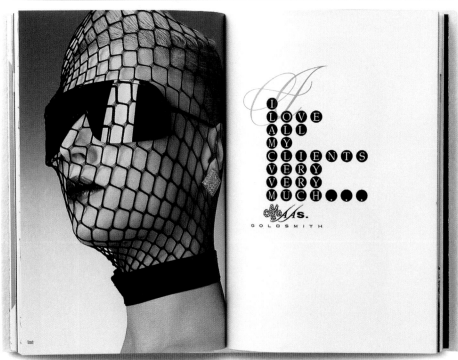

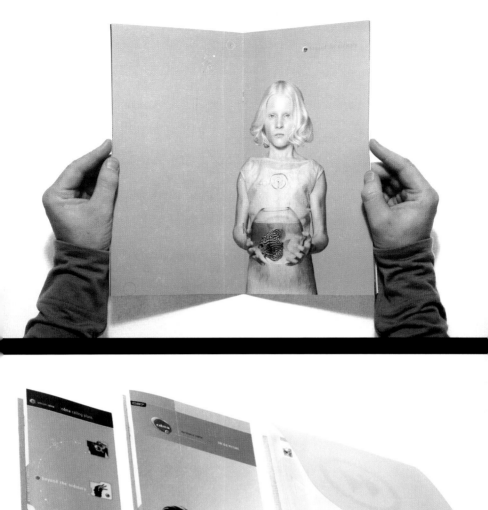

<What this country needs is a really good 5-cents cigar.>

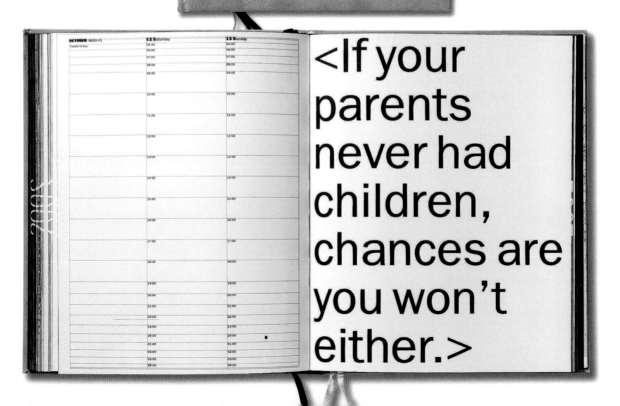

<If your parents never had children, chances are you won't either.>

(this spread) Design Firm: Esther Noyons Designers: Esther Noyons and K. v. d. Eerden Photographers: B. v. d. Biezen and H. Oerlemans Illustrator: Layla Curtis Copywriter: Maaike Bleeker Client: Ando br.

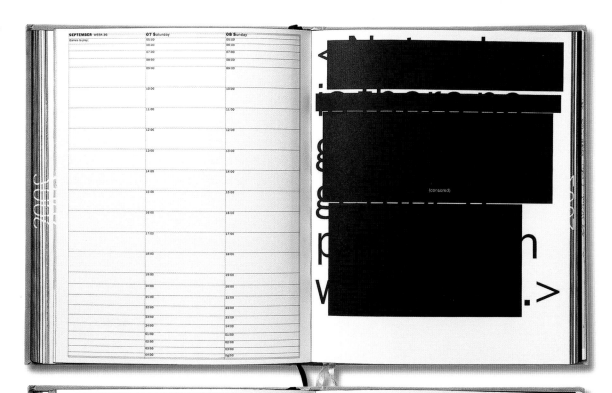

Deze agenda is een initiatief van
Drukkerij Ando, Den Haag

Concept/grafisch ontwerp >
Katrien van der Eerden +
Esther Noyons, Amsterdam

Selectie citaten >
Maaike Bleeker, Amsterdam

Foto 'Euro–presentatie' >
WFA/Bram van de Biezen, Nunspeet
Foto 'Schommelend Meisje' >
Hester Oerlemans, Berlijn
Kaart 'World Political' >
Layla Curtis (laylacurtis.com)
c/o Rhodes + Mann, Londen

Druk >
Ando bv, Den Haag (Roland 705 +
Roland 305 + Speedmaster)

Afwerking >
Binderij Bosboom, Den Haag +
Binderij Stokkink, Amsterdam

Papier binnenwerk >
Tollius 140 gr/m², houtvrij offset
Grafisch Papier, Andelst

Lettertype >
Franklin Gothic

© Ando bv
Niets van deze uitgave mag worden verveelvoudigd en/of openbaar gemaakt door middel van druk, fotokopie,
microfilm of op welke andere wijze ook, zonder voorafgaande schriftelijke toestemming van de uitgever.

Ando bv > Mercuriusweg 37 > 2516 AW Den Haag
T (070) 385 07 08 > F (070) 385 07 09 > E ando@ando.net > I www.ando.net

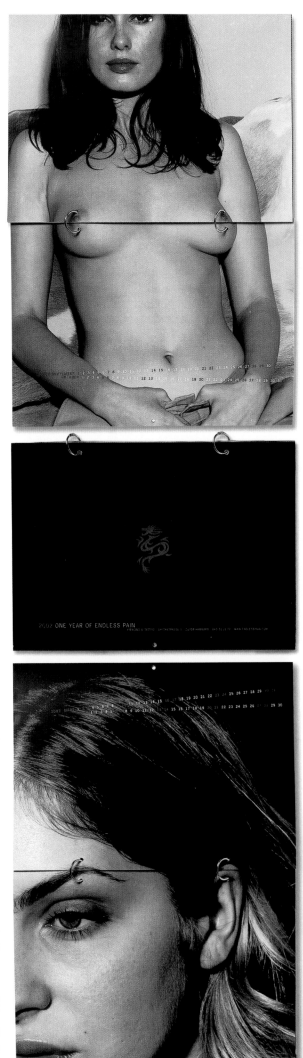

'Endless Pain' Design Firm: Weigertpirouzwolf Creative Directors: Michael Reissinger and Kay Eichner Art Director: Barbara Schirmer Photographer: Hans Starck Copywriter: Kay Eichner Client: Endless Pain Tattoo & Piercing Company

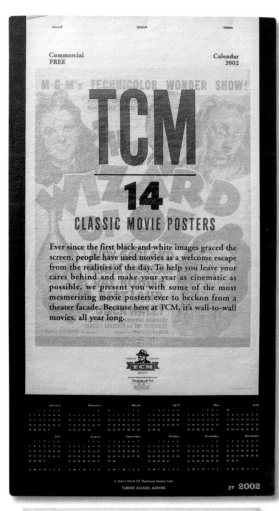

Design Firm: Templin Brink Design Creative Director: Joel Templin Art Director: Joel Templin Designer: Joel Templin Client: Turner Classic Movies Calendars 58,59

(this spread) Design Firm: Vanderbyl Design Creative Director: Michael Vanderbyl Art Director: Michael Vanderbyl Designers: Michael Vanderbyl and Karin Myint Photographers: Todd Hido and Douglas Sandberg Copywriter: Mindpower, Inc. Client: California College of Arts & Crafts

"I entered CCAC as a ceramics major, but switched to photography because it offered me a greater sense of personal expression. For me, the camera became an intimate creative vehicle—one that allowed me to explore unfamiliar terrain. Now, I use it as an excuse to do things I wouldn't ordinarily do, and to look at things I wouldn't ordinarily have access to. Despite the comfort level, I have to admit that photography is less instinctive for me than ceramics. After I took a writing and image-making class with Larry Sultan, I began to experiment with storytelling, exploring different ways to manipulate a picture book by the sequencing and pacing of my images. After CCAC, I'd like to try commercial photography before I enter graduate school in New York or London."

photography   natalie cartwright

4th year

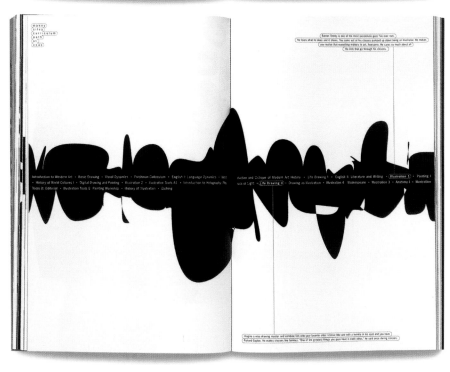

Introduction to Western Art • Basic Drawing • Visual Dynamics • Freshman Colloquium • English I: Language Dynamics • Intro   duction and Critique of Modern Art History • Life Drawing I • English 3: Literature and Writing • Illustration 1 • Painting 1 • History of World Cultures I • Digital Drawing and Painting • Illustration 2 • Illustration Tools A1 • Introduction to Printmaking: Pho   ics of Light • Life Drawing II • Drawing as Illustration • Illustration 4 • Shakespeare • Illustration 3 • Anatomy I • Illustration   Tools D: Editorial • Illustration Tools E: Painting Workshop • History of Illustration • Etching

(this spread) 'Björn Dahlström Catalog' Design Firm: Happy Forsman & Bodenfors Creative Director: Anders Kornesedt Art Director: Andreas Kittel Photographers: Joakim Bergström, Ake Eison Lindman, Bjorn Keller and Mathias Pettersson Copywriters: Ulf Beckman

RÖHSSKA MUSEETS KATALOG NR. 8 FÖR

Torsten och Wanja Söderbergs pris

BJÖRN DAHLSTRÖM

NORDISKT DESIGN- OCH KONSTHANTVERKSPRIS 2001

RÖHSSKA MUSEET

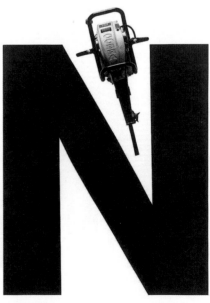

RÖHSSKA MUSEET

Lousby later founded the Växjö School of Animation (Animationsskolan i Växjö), which is now one of the courses at the Swedish University College of Arts, Crafts and Design (Konstfack). Dahlström would almost certainly have applied for this course if it had existed, but there were no animation courses whatsoever in Sweden at that time. Making cartoons was a natural continuation of the 14 year-old Dahlström's intensive font design project. One second of animated film consists of 24 drawings. The mechanical precision involved in making cartoons is self-evident: 1,440 frames are required for a minute's animation. Today, most this work is done on computers, but in the 70s, animated films were still made completely by hand. Work as animated cartoonist must have been an excellent training for eye-hand coordination, the ability to reproduce an image with strict precision. The same line must be drawn again and again, with minuscule adjustments. The depth of the picture must be similarly adjusted to achieve the desired illusion of plasticity. Creating images by hand in this way is a dying art; computers do it faster and with greater precision. In 1978, Dahlström, now just over 20 years old, became the art director of an advertising agency (Marknadsinitiativ, later renamed Gurbergs). There he tried his hand at advertisements, where his knowledge of animation, film tricks and cartoons proved extremely useful. Regarding today's computer-aided drawing methods, he stresses how much he has benefited from his experience in animation, not least when working with graphic design for presentation material, instruction manuals and videos, which many of today's companies use to market the products they design. Computers are a fantastic tool that collects and stores the elements of the design, which can then be (re)used for these very purposes. To Dahlström, this means coming full circle: he can return to animation without it being too time-consuming.

However, Björn Dahlström was not entirely content with the world of advertising. It did not satisfy his need for something more anchored in reality, something permanent that would serve a wider public and could be used from a longer perspective. He was looking for something else. Consequently, in 1981, he branched out alone and moved into his own studio. Four years later, he transferred to a studio that he furnished himself. However, he did not yet attempt to design furniture. He did not feel ready to start designing products, even though this appealed to him. So he continued with graphic design, working for several major companies including Atlas Copco Berema, Ericsson and Scania. The contacts he made then would later prove extremely valuable when the time came to move on. After a few years, Dahlström transferred to larger premises with space for more people. In 1991, he was joined by the graphic designer Henrik Nygren, a good friend and peer who was self-trained like Dahlström. Nygren had also learned the trade through hands-on experience. He had progressed from artist to Art Director at a number of advertising agencies, but now wanted to work for himself. This friendship and working relationship with Nygren was extremely important to Björn Dahlström. Their daily contact lead to continuous discussions on style and design, attitudes and ideas. There were never any competitive barriers between them. Nygren was fully geared towards a career in graphic design, while Dahlström was moving towards product design. Their friendship and collaboration has lasted right up to the present. For instance, Henrik Nygren designed the catalogues for Dahlström's exhibitions at the Felleshus of the Nordic Embassies in Berlin in 2000, and at the Museum of Science & Technology in Stockholm in 2001. By 1995, Björn Dahlström's business had expanded. He had taken on several new employees, and the studio was now too small. Henrik Nygren moved to his own premises and Dahlström opened his present design studio in Sibirien, an area in northern central Stockholm. Dahlström Design is renovating its space to accommodate its six employees. In 1999, Dahlström was appointed Professor of Furniture Design at the University College of Arts, Crafts and Design in Stockholm, a position that he has reluctantly chosen to give up after barely a year. He feels he needs to prioritise his own design work at the moment, in the best interests of both himself and his students. Regarding design schools, he feels that much of a designer's technical expertise can be gained independently through practical experience, apprenticeship etc., while a school can offer a "foundation kit" for future design activities. It gives the students a theoretical grounding and helps them develop basic working methods, serving as a bridge to the profession. Today's Swedish design schools produce many excellent designers, and are easily on a par with the best international schools.

As we have already mentioned, all Björn Dahlström's designs (and his output is considerable) are based on a graphic approach. This is particularly evident in his furniture designs, which are worth taking a closer look at from this perspective. Even his early furniture designs, which include a table with a cast iron foot from the late 80s, are clearly characterised by graphic geometry. Notice the straight lines, the circles and the quadrangles that make up these designs. He may not have used these shapes more than other designers to begin with, but soon he added the simple curve and the triangle, which gradually break away from the geometric plane and assume their own asymmetry. This applies to BD 1, a stuffed, upholstered chair from 1994, often referred to as "the cotton". A simple block, parallel piped for a correct image, is here into a carefully calculated sitting angle and supported by a frame with four equally simple block-shaped legs. At first glance, these legs may appear too thick for the design, but in fact they are perfectly proportioned to the style of the chair and its sturdy appearance, giving the viewer a clear impression that this chair will not readily break or tip over. BD 1 (or Small Armchair, as it was called while Dahlström was producing it himself) is one of the clearest examples of his way of adapting graphic form to three-dimensional design. His aims was to create a soft chair, an armchair if you like, as small and compact as possible while still remaining comfortable. It was to be fully upholstered, based on graphic black with a typograp

42

BD 5 FRÅN 1997. TILLVERKARE: CBI, STOCKHOLM.
MATERIAL: FORMPRESSAD STOMME MED POLYESTERSTOPPNING OCH
KLÄDSEL AV YLLETYG. UNDERREDE AV KROMADE STÅLRÖR.

BD 5 FROM 1997. MANUFACTURER: CBI, STOCKHOLM.
MATERIALS: COMPRESSION MOULDED SHELL AND HIGH DENSITY FOAM
STUFFING, WITH A WOOLLEN COVER. FRAME OF CHROMED STEEL TUBE.

BD 1 FRÅN 1994. TILLVERKARE: CBI, STOCKHOLM. MATERIAL: SITTKORG
I FORMPRESSAD BJÖRK MED LAGER AV KALLSKUM. BENSTÄLLNING I
BJÖRK OCH KLÄDSEL I YLLETYG. DENNA FÅTÖLJ VAR BÖRJAN TILL ETT
FLERTAL TJOCKBÄTSIGA MÖBLER I SAMMA ANDA.

BD 1 FROM 1994. MANUFACTURER: CBI, STOCKHOLM. MATERIALS: SHELL
OF COMPRESSION MOULDED BIRCH, COVERED WITH SEVERAL LAYERS OF
HIGH DENSITY FOAM, LEGS OF BIRCH. UPHOLSTED IN WOOLEN MATERIAL.
THIS ARMCHAIR WAS THE FIRST OF SEVERAL THICK-SEATED ITEMS OF
FURNITURE IN THE SAME STYLE.

(this spread) Design Firm: Design M:W Creative Director: Allison Williams Art Director: Allison Williams Designers: Yael Eisele and Allison Williams Photographer: Gentl & Hyers Copywriter: Laura Silverman Client: Takashimaya New York

Sex appeal is virtually indefinable. It has something to do with smell. Or is it touch? A bare shoulder, a whiff of musk, and the fantasy comes to life. . . . NECKLACE Wendy Brigode's exquisite strand of brown and bronze freshwater pearls is mixed with red tiger's eye and finished at each end with a chunk of smoky topaz. Wrap it around several sultry times, wear it long or loop it as a lariat. 60", $650 [61]. . . . FRAGRANCE Our sophisticated signature scent, t by Takashimaya, incorporates the intoxicating aromas of jasmine, muguet, orange flower, tea and cedarwood with hints of amber, sandalwood and patchouli. The result is beautifully balanced between refined and reckless. Left to right: moisturizer, 8 oz., $25 [71]; small candle, 4 oz. $25 [70]; large candle, 8 oz., $45 [70]; esprit de parfum, 3.4 oz. $75 [70]; parfum, 1 oz. $125 [70]. Not shown: boxed soap, set of 3, $18 [70]; shower gel, 8 oz., $25 [70]; body mist spray, 8 oz. $25 [70].

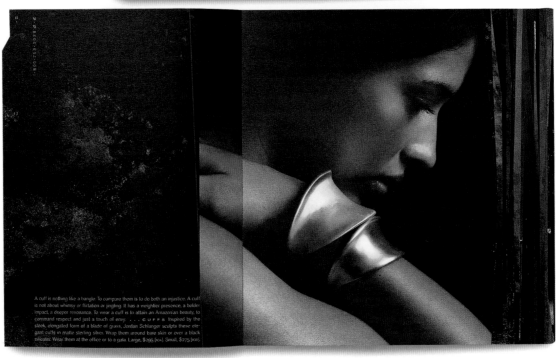

A cuff is nothing like a bangle. To compare them is to do both an injustice. A cuff is not about whimsy or flirtation or jingling. It has a weightier presence, a bolder impact, a deeper resonance. To wear a cuff is to attain an Amazonian beauty, to command respect and just a touch of envy. . . . CUFFS Inspired by the sleek, elongated form of a blade of grass, Jordan Schlanger sculpts these elegant cuffs in matte sterling silver. Wrap them around bare skin or over a black sweater. Wear them at the office or to a gala. Large, $295 [104]. Small, $275 [108].

Get a grip. A good one comes in handy, whether you're shaking hands or swinging a nine iron, dancing a tango or hanging on for dear life. Cultivate a firm grasp of the important things in life, lest you let them slip through your fingers. . . . **LADLES** Hand-hammered aluminum ladles are useful for both cooking and serving. In fact, they can dish out everything but good advice, from sangria to stew. For easy gripping, the handles are wrapped with akebia vine. Japan. Hand wash. 11.8", $35 [194]. 7.8", $22 [198]. 10", $35 [19C]. 9.2", $25 [190].

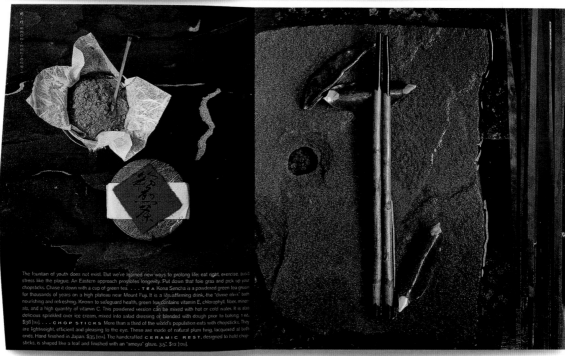

The fountain of youth does not exist. But we've learned new ways to prolong life: eat right, exercise, avoid stress like the plague. An Eastern approach promotes longevity. Put down that foie gras and pick up your chopsticks. Chase it down with a cup of green tea. . . . **TEA** Kona Sencha is a powdered green tea grown for thousands of years on a high plateau near Mount Fuji. It is a life-affirming drink, the "divine elixir" both nourishing and refreshing. Known to safeguard health, green tea contains vitamin E, chlorophyll, fiber, minerals, and a high quantity of vitamin C. This powdered version can be mixed with hot or cold water. It is also delicious sprinkled over ice cream, mixed into salad dressing or blended with dough prior to baking. 1 oz. $38 [19A]. . . . **CHOPSTICKS** More than a third of the world's population eats with chopsticks. They are lightweight, efficient and pleasing to the eye. These are made of natural plum twig, lacquered at both ends. Hand finished in Japan. $35 [19A]. The handcrafted **CERAMIC REST**, designed to hold chopsticks, is shaped like a leaf and finished with an "ameyu" glaze. 3.5", $12 [19B].

GROOMING Czech & Speake, the venerable English house of toiletries, named this fragrance No. 88 after its original Jermyn Street location in London. It is a complex scent with a distinctly masculine character; composed of cassis, rose, bergamot and geranium set against a warm, woodsy base of vetiver and sandalwood. From left: triple-milled moisturizing soap, 75 gm. $13 [48A]; bath essential oil, 100 mL, $56 [48B]; large shaving brush, made of finest white badger hair, $84 [48C]; shaving soap with glycerin and coconut oil, 90 gm, and dish, $89 [48D]; soothing aftershave gel 60 gm, $54 [48E]. Also available, cologne spray, 100 mL, $83 [48F]. . . . **BAGS** Valextra doesn't fool around. Its Italian leather bags are considered to be the very best available, and are created in numbered, limited edition series. Beautifully designed and crafted of the finest materials, they boast internationally patented hardware features, including a combination lock, money clips, and special closures. The black leather doctor bag has a hidden leather flap that zips on top for a boxy, roomier look; two inside storage pockets and one inside zip compartment. Fully lined with Valextra's understated green-logo fabric. 20.5" x 13" x 10.5", $1595 [49A]. The Arietta is a small black leather suitcase, ideal for short trips. It has two inside compartments, divider pad; outside pockets; reinforced corners; and 5 rolling studs on the bottom. Comes with matching luggage tag. 17.75" x 13.75" x 7", $2850 [49B]. . . . **SHOEHORN** Step lively. Nickel shoe horn folds up to fit neatly into its black leather case. Italy. $55 [50A].

What do gentlemen prefer? If only the answer were simply "blondes". It seems to be a great deal more complicated. So we've gone out of our way to come up with some compelling choices for even the most discriminating.

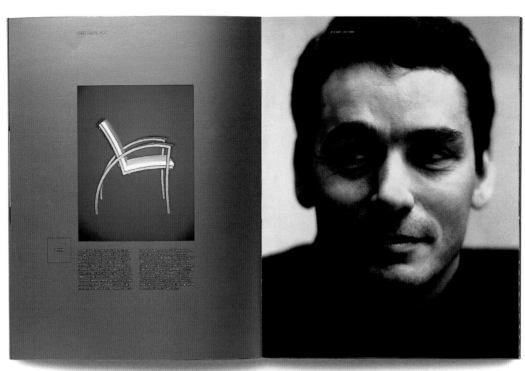

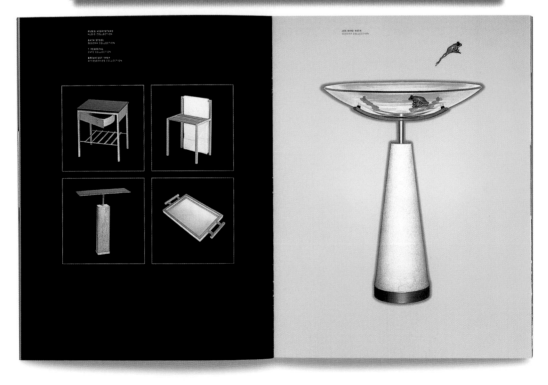

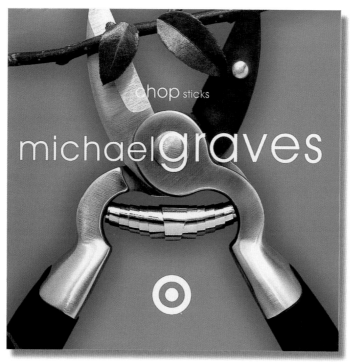

visit us in-store or at target.com

home grown design

Don't be surprised to find yourself spending more and more time outdoors. With a new line of garden tools and accessories, Michael Graves has masterfully brought his inner style outside, and made the garden a new center of leisure and entertainment. These products are anything but garden variety.

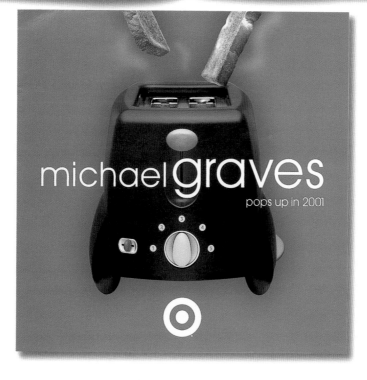

Design Firm: Design Guys Creative Director: Steven Sikora Art Director: Steven Sikora Copywriter: Jay Kaskel Client: Target Corporation   Catalogues 66,67

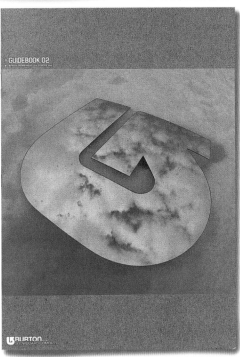

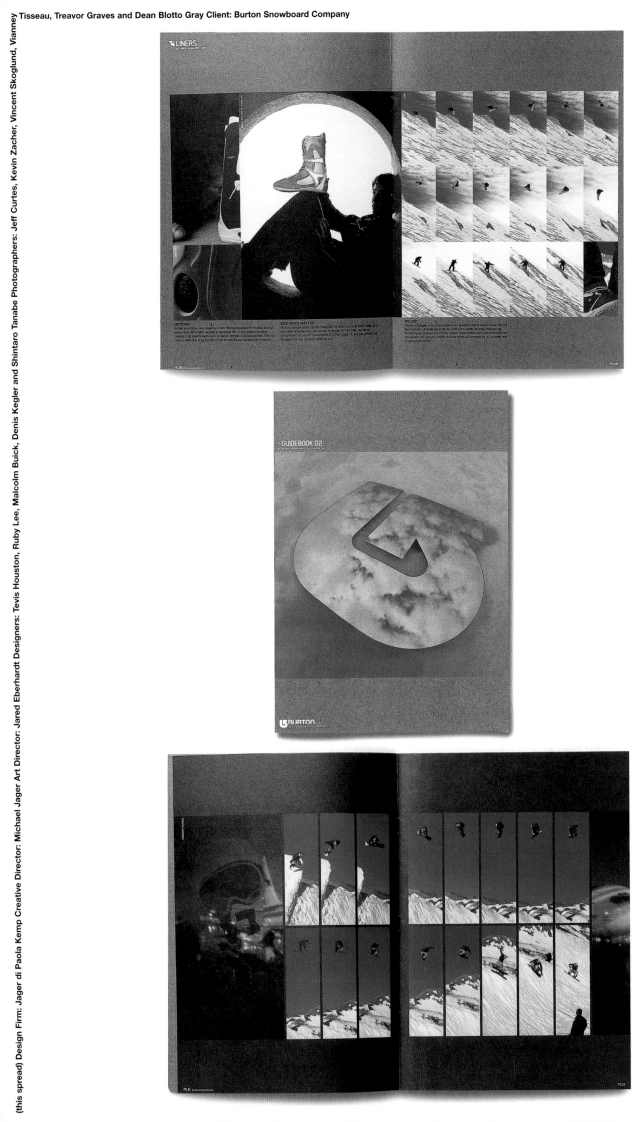

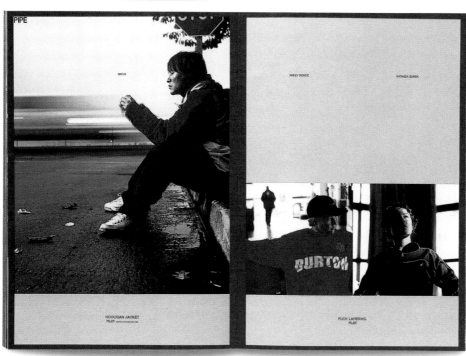

Design Firm: Nike Brand Design Creative Directors: John Hoke and Greg Hoffman Art Director: David Odusanya Designers: Satoru Igarashi, Adam Cohn, Scott Patt Glenn Geisendorfer and David McLaughlin Copywriters: Dennie Wendt and Cory Hansen Client: Nike

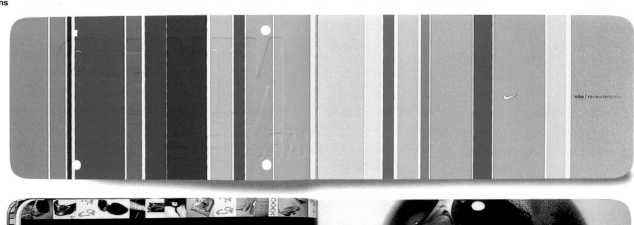

This is the shoe that changed the way athletic shoes are made.

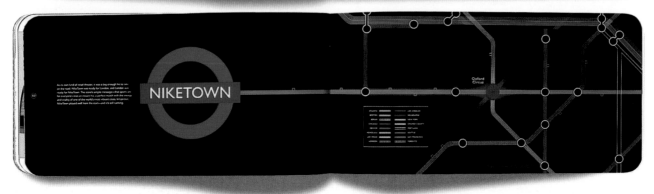

NIKETOWN

Design Firm: Vanderbyl Design Creative Director: Michael Vanderbyl Art Director: Michael Vanderbyl Designers: Michael Vanderbyl and Erica Wilcott Photographer: Jim Hedrich Copywriter: Penny Benda Client: Teknion Inc.

Catalogues 70, 71

'Design Does Matter' & 'Teknion xm'

Firm: Taku Satoh Design Office, Inc. Art Director: Taku Satoh Designers: Taku Satoh and Shino Misawa Photographer: Ayumi Okubo Client: Japan Design Committee

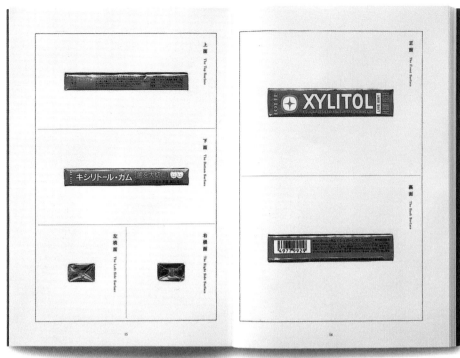

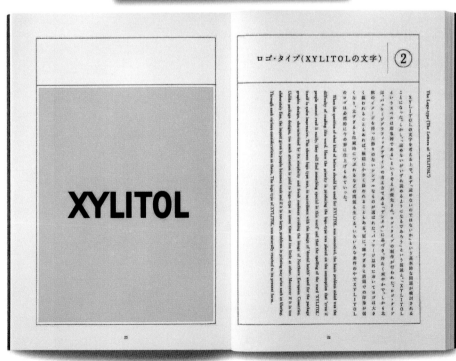

(this spread) 'Analysis of the Mass Product Design for Lotte's "Xylitol" Chewing Gum' Design Firm: Taku Satoh Design Office, Inc. Art Director: Taku Satoh Designers: Taku Satoh and Shino Misawa Photographer: Ayumi Okubo Client: Japan Design Committee

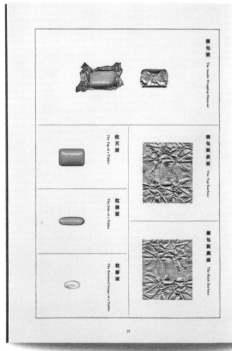

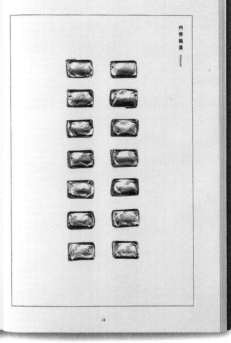

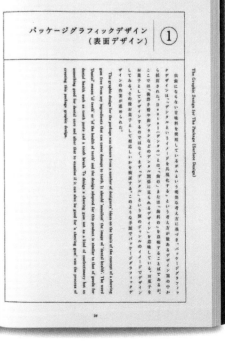

GREASY BATTER

GB

LAGER MADE FOR GREAT BRITAIN
ABV 4.2%

GLOOMY BEACHES

GB

LAGER MADE FOR GREAT BRITAIN
ABV 4.2%

GNOME BONKERS

GB

LAGER MADE FOR GREAT BRITAIN
ABV 4.2%

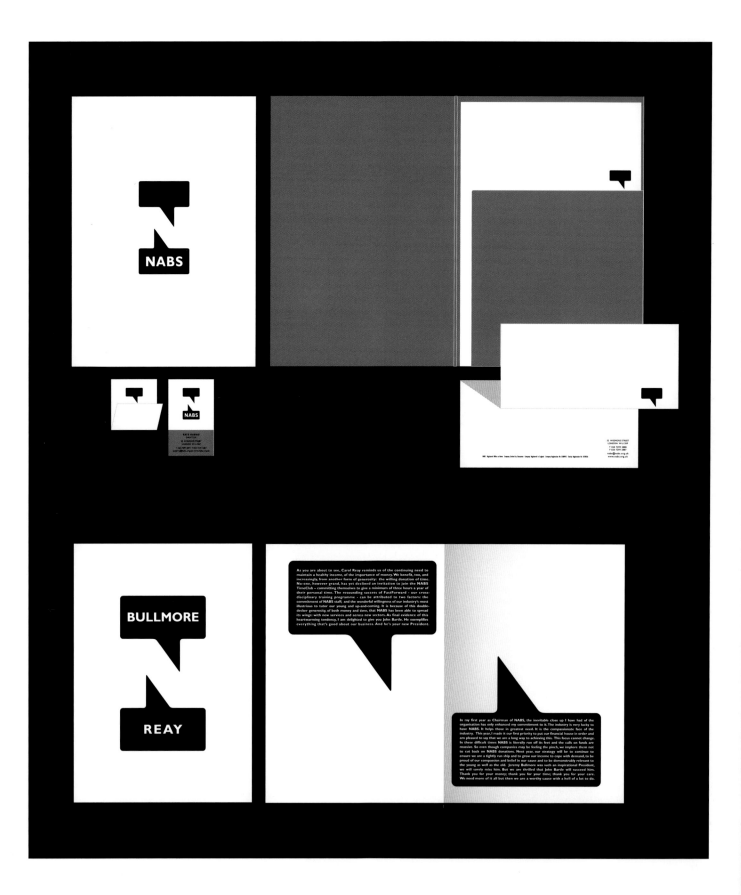

(this spread) Design Firm: Lewis Moberly Art Director: Mary Lewis Designer: Paul Cilia La Corte Client: NABS

MANY

THANKS

to everyone who contributed time & money, especially 141 Communications, 24/7 Media UK, AAR Group, Abbott Mead Vickers, BBDO, ACT, Active International, ADCOM Group, Adplates Group, Advertising Standards Authority, AKQA, Alchemy, All Response Media, AMRA, AMS Media, Archibald Ingall Stretton, Ashurst Ogilvy Crisp, Associated Newspapers, Attic Futura, Auto Trader, Autocar, Banks Hoggins O'Shea FCB, Bartle Bogle Hegarty, Bates UK, BBC, BBH Unlimited, BBJ Media, BHWG Proximity, Billett Consultancy, BJK & E, Bloomberg, Blue 10, BMP DDB, BMP Interaction, Brad Group, Breathe.com, Brilliant Independent Media Specialists, British Television Awards, BSkyB, Burkitt DDB, C W Communications, Campaign, Campden Publishing, Capital Radio Advertising, Carat, Caribiner International, Carlson, Carlton Digital, Carlton TV, Carney Richardson, Carpetright Plc, CDP, Centaur Publishing, Channel 4, Channel 5, Chime Communications, Chris Dickens Communications, CIA Manchester, CIA UK Ltd, Citrus Publishing, Clark McKay & Walpole, CNN, Communications Agency, Communications Unit, Conrad Advertising, Craik Jones Watson Mitchell Voelkel, Cravens Advertising, Creative Circle, Creative Review, Cursitor Street Lunch, D&AD, D'Arcy, Daily Mail, Daily Record, Daily Telegraph, Deepend, Delaney Lund Knox Warren, Design Week, Digitas, DLA, DLKW, Doner Cardwell Hawkins, Double Column Club, Doubleclick, Duckworth Finn Grubb Waters, Economist, Economist Charitable Trust, ehsrealtime, EMAP Advertising, Empire Design, Enterprise IG, Euro RSCG Direct, Euro RSCG Wnek Gosper, Evening Standard, Express Newspapers, Fairbrother Media Ltd, Fallon London Limited, Fast Forward Hosts, Speakers and Delegates, Feather Brooksbank, FileFX, Financial Times, First Friday Club, Fish4, Flextech, Flicks, Frame Store, Freight Media, Fullers, Future News, General Management Committee, Geographical Magazine, GMTV, Granada Enterprises, Grey Worldwide, Guardian Media Group, Harrison Troughton Wunderman, Haymarket Publishing, HHCL & Partners, Hub Communications Group, Hyway Printing Group, iMediapoint.com, IMP London, Impact, Independent Newspapers (UK), Independent Direct Marketing, Independent Magazines, Informa, Initiative Media, Interfocus, International Advertising Association UK Chapter, IPA, IPC Media, Iris, ITV, J Walter Thompson, Jane Fuller Associates, JCDecaux, John Brown Publishing, Johnston Press plc, Joshua, Keene Group, Kelland Communications, Ladbrokes, Lastminute.com, Lavery Rowe Advertising, Leagas Delaney Group, Leo Burnett, Lewis Moberly, Loot, Lowe Lintas, M&C Saatchi, Mad.co.uk, Maiden Outdoor, Mail Marketing International, Mail on Sunday, Manning Gottlieb Media, Mansfield Lang Direct, MarketForce (UK) Ltd, Marketing, Marketing Drive, MBS Media Limited, McCann Erickson, Media Business, Media Shop Scotland, Media Week, Mediacom, Mediatel, MediaVest (Manchester), Melarno Media, Men's Health, Metro, Miles Calcraft Briginshaw Duffy, MindShare, Mirror Colour Print, Money Extra, More Group UK, MPA, MPA 250 Club, MPA Golf Club, MRI International, Mullis Morgan Imaging, NABS Manchester Committee, NAGS, National Magazines Company, Nelson Bostock, New PHD, News Group Newspapers, News International, News Stream, Nexus Media Ltd, Ogilvy, OMD UK, Open Interactive, OPMA, Optimedia UK, Organic, Oyez Straker, PACE, Page3.com, Payroll Givers, Periodical Publishers Association, Personal donors, Personnel Publications Ltd, Perspectives, Peter White, Polestar Group, Poolside, Poster Publicity, Posterscope, Primesight, Publicis, Publicity Club of Glasgow, Quokka, Rainey Kelly Campbell Roalfe/Y&R, Rapids Group Plc, Rapier Ltd, Red Rox Sports, Redwood Group, Rocket, RE&A, Ron Miller, Roose & Partners, Saatchi & Saatchi, Saints & Sinners, Sales Promotion, Scottish Daily Record, Scottish Outdoor Advertising Social Group, Seven Worldwide, Siegelgale, Silicon.com, Solus Club, Songseekers International, Sports.com, St Brides Fleet Street, St Ives Web Ltd, St Michaels Press, Starcom Motive, Stora Enso, Syzygy, TalkSPORT, TargetNM, TBWA\London, TDI Media, Team LGM, Telegraph Group, Tequila London, The Adwomen, The Partners, Time Club Members, Times Newspapers, Trinity Mirror, Turner Broadcasting, UKAMS, Universal McCann, UPM-Kymmene Ltd, Vassat Broadcasting, Virgin Radio, VLP, VNU, WACL, Walker Media, Walsh Trott Chick Smith, Warman and Bannister, WCRS, Welfare Committees A and B, Which?, Willox Ambler Rodford Law, WPP, Wunderman Cato Johnson, WWAV Rapp Collins Media, Yattendon Investment Trust, Yellow Submarine and Zenith Media

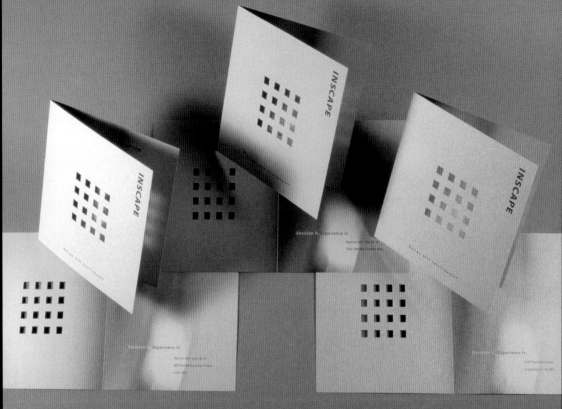

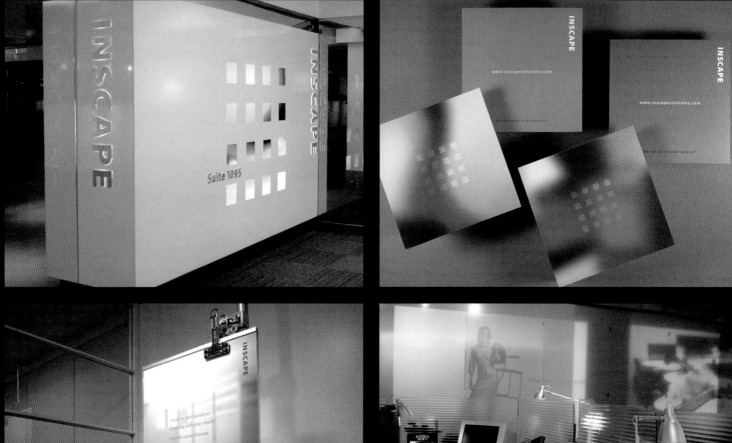

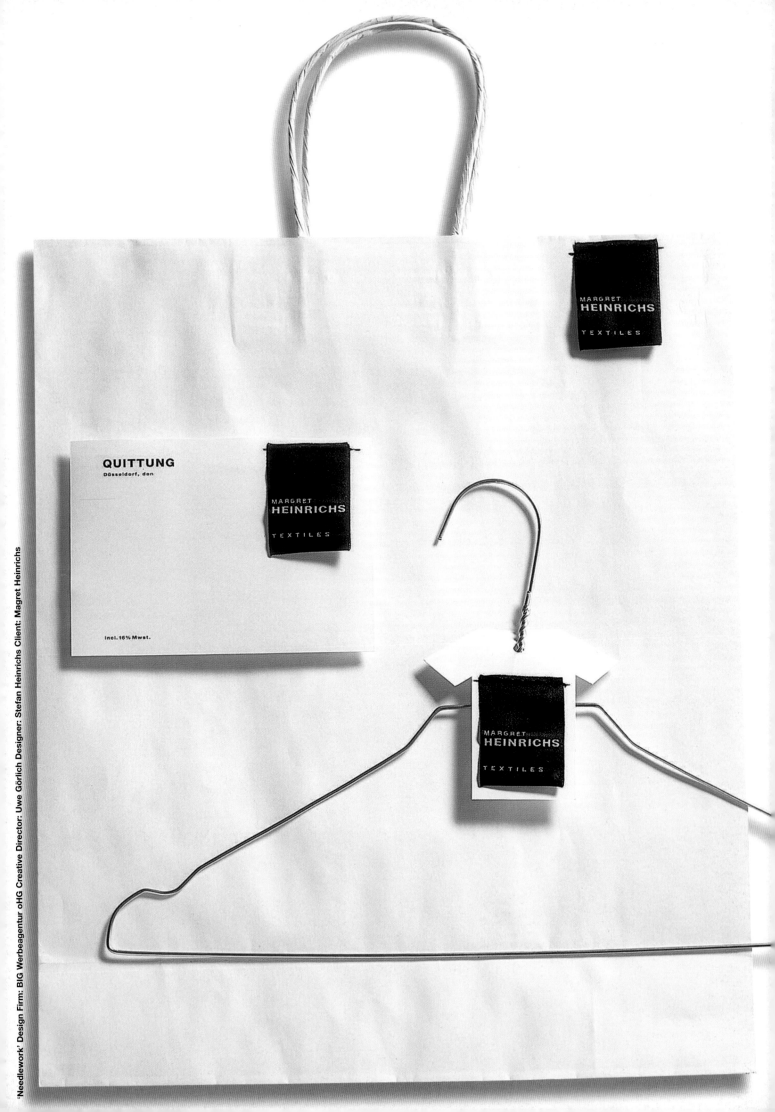

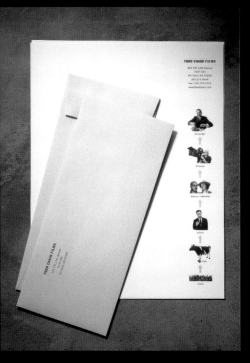

(this spread) Design Firm: Haefelinger Wagner Design Creative Director: Frank Wanger Art Directors: Th. Häussler and Th. Tscherter Designer: Th. Fing Client: Power One   Corporate Identity 84,85

(t)here

ISSUE 5
US $10.00 Canada $12.00

and cultural debates were trying to promote and preserve: a field in which even the innovative force of futurism had resulted in no more than a contamination of formal and decorative styles and repertoires.

In reality, the opening up to a new kind of design in this field came in the early thirties, following the discussions of these themes carried in the pages of two magazines, "Domus" and "La casa bella," which had commenced publication in 1928: discussions that, like futurism took a totally ideological approach to the industrial world. As did Edoardo Persico when he spoke of the "aesthetics of the machine," citing a motor-powered ship or a Savoia Marchetti airplane as examples. Yet, they were also open to wholly innovative modes of design, of clearly functionalistic and rationalistic origin, that were not slow in producing absolutely extraordinary results. It is no coincidence that in 1930, then in 1930 the "International Biennial exhibition of Decorative Arts" in Monza changed its name to the "International Triennial Exhibition of Modern Decorative and Industrial Arts." And the presentation of the "Electric House" at this exhibition further underlined what was by now an unstoppable shift toward the acceptance of modern ideas.

The idea of the record seems to have been a constant or characterising element in much of Italian industrial design. It was an approach to design in which given the mode of operation, doubts have to be raised about its industrial character, owning up the dominance of a dimension very different from what is traditionally considered industrial (one lined more as a particular way of designing and producing) and the pleasure that was taken in pushing the limits of the possible rather than striving to be a significant actor in the world of manufacturing and commerce.

Piaggio M1C 81-90 FO. Trev. 1936

Caproni Campini Aircraft, C.C. No 1. 1940 Design by Secondo Campini

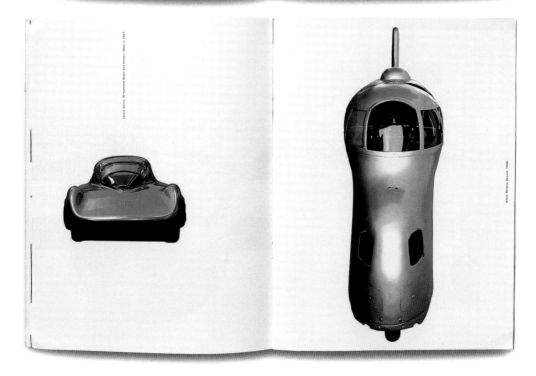

Lancia Aprilia. Streamlined Sedan 2nd Version. Made in 1937

Gliera Nireoni Record. 1935

S O U N D

made up of vibrations, is energy.
To release the energy from the sound,
we learn to repeat it as a certain rhythm.
When you repeat a Mantra,
it creates a specific thought pattern.
The energy literally manifests itself.

pictures salvador calvano
words master sivananda

New Orleans, Louisiana   B A S I N   S T R E E T

pictures mark andrew words gina crozier clothes jim smiley/vintage clothing - new orleans contributing editor johnny gambitsky

Woonmode

Name and form are like
two sides of a coin; you cannot
have one without the other.
When you repeat a name,
form comes to mind.
The thought patterns created
by the Mantras are positive
beneficial, calming ones.

NIMJAB, India

dutch style company
perscentrum wonen
monique van der reijden
marcello gimenes
saskia ten cate

pictures: jan luijt

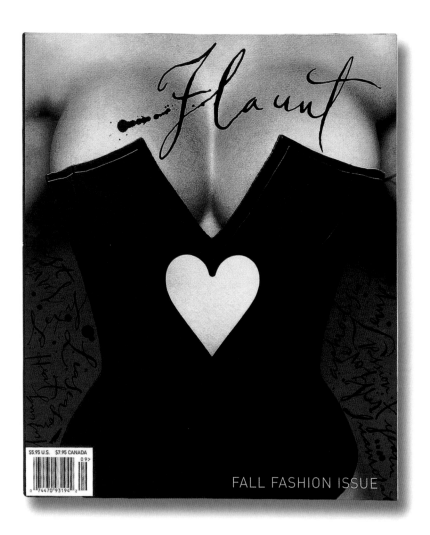

FALL FASHION ISSUE

$5.95 U.S. $7.95 CANADA

Frog in "Ophidian Texture" wallpaper from **Schumacher**. Background in "Lawn Cavallo 901/Dinosaur" leather wall tiles from **Gaetlina Leathers** (212) 463-7845.

Ornament designed by Molly Kahn in "Rutledge Plaid" wallpaper from **Schumacher**. Background in "Erera Chilopaper" vinyl wallcovering from **Wolf-Gordon Inc.**

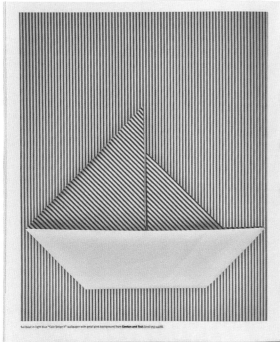

Sailboat in Light Blue "Gale Stripe II" wallpaper with petal pink background from **Cowtan and Tout** (212) 753-4488.

Thai flower and leaf in "Kehai" wallpaper from **Clarence House** and stem in "Sylvan Toile" wallpaper from **Greeff Fabrics** (888) 298-2990. Background in "Thebes" wallpaper from **J.R. Burrows & Company** (781) 982-1812.

Butterflies designed by Michael LaFosse in "Kehai" wallpaper from **Clarence House**. Background in "Tropique" wallpaper from **Schumacher**.

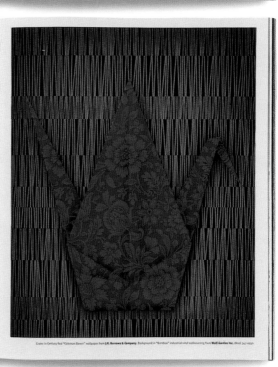

Crane in Century Red "Coleman Dover" wallpaper from **J.R. Burrows & Company**. Background in "Bamboo" industrial vinyl wallcovering from **Wolf-Gordon Inc.** (800) 347-0550.

Harper's

BAZZAAR

635 Fashion ideas

Shop like an expert

Best beauty buys

Must-have bags

Essential pieces

Style solutions

Hot, sexy stilettos

FIND your
New
Look
What to wear now

FEBRUARY $3.00

02

0 754724 7

HARPERSBAZAAR.COM

Harper's

BAZZAAR

Fashion's back!

Take the plunge. THIS
PAGE: Resin inter-cut
bag, $775, Giorgio
Armani. Lacquered mini
bangle, $65, R.J.
Graziano. OPPOSITE
PAGE: Patent-leather
ankle-wrap sandal,
$260, Calvin Klein. See
Where to Buy for details.
Fashion editor:
Mary Alice Stephenson

Dive into the wet look with lacquered cuffs,
patent-leather sandals, and iridescent clutches.
Photographed by Hiro

KISS

Instant
attraction:
The return of
romantic red
lips and eye
shadow that
shimmers.
Photographed by
Solve Sundsbo

TRUE LOVE
The sheer red lip from
years past gets softer
for spring, thanks to sweet,
flexible colors and textures.
Telephone Lipstick in
Rose Galore $18, Calvin
Klein. More Than Mascara
in Too Black $17.50,
and Skin All Day Natural
Eyeshadow in Blossom
$17.50, all, Estée Lauder.
See Where to Buy for details.
Beauty editor:
Charlotte Stockdale

And we all shine on...
THIS PAGE: Leather wrist
wallet, $330, Helmut
Lang. Cuff, $75, Couttie
Malouf for Michael Kors.
OPPOSITE PAGE: Patent-
leather sandal, $360,
Michael Kors. The
portfolio. Manicure:
Bernadette Thompson for
bernadettethompson.com.
See Where to Buy
for details.
BEAUTY BAZAAR
Protect your hands from
the elements with
Lancôme Nutri-Source
Intensive Refreshing
Hand Treatment with
SPF 15, $25.

A solo update on Botticelli's Le Primavera: whimsy, beauty, and an enchanting garden-print dress. Dress, $4370, Louis Vuitton. Select Louis Vuitton stores. See Where to Buy for details.

By Lichtenstein's Kiss, princess is laid bedside. Bra a polka-dot suit. $95, Ralph Lauren Swimwear, Lord & Taylor, NYC. See Where to Buy for details.

BEAUTY BAZAAR
When going to bright red lips, make sure the colors can handle intense matte saturation in Chili Matte Lipstick, $15, M.A.C. Clay Matte Lipstick, $8.25, and Lancôme Matte Dry Red Lipstick in Acilrace, $21, Avon. See Where to Buy for details.

Cancan into the spotlight with sassiness à la Toulouse-Lautrec in a sexy corset dress. Silk spotted dress, $1000, Alexander McQueen. Feathered hat, $1250, Kokin. By special order at Bergdorf Goodman, NYC. See Where to Buy for details.

Cuddle up, Koons-style, with the bare necessities—golden skin and a bold bikini. Lycra boy-shorts, $85, Eres. Eres, NYC. Pink panther made by Karen Fitzpatrick for Design Support. See Where to Buy for details.

BEAUTY BAZAAR
Keep sexy waves in place with Clairol Herbal Essences Extra Hold Hairspray, $2.95.

Modigliani's sculptural style is matched with a fitted top and full skirt. Sheer jersey ruched top, $195, Donna Karan New York. Select Neiman Marcus stores. Suede peasant skirt, $958, Bluffo, Louis Boston, Boston. See Where to Buy for details.

Balenciaga raises the gold standard with a bohemian update of Gustav Klimt's The Kiss. Pleated chiffon apron dress, $600, Balenciaga. Neiman Marcus, San Francisco. Cuffon: Cape, Bridget Costumes; Urban Metal wall covering from Blumenthal Inc. See Where to Buy for details.

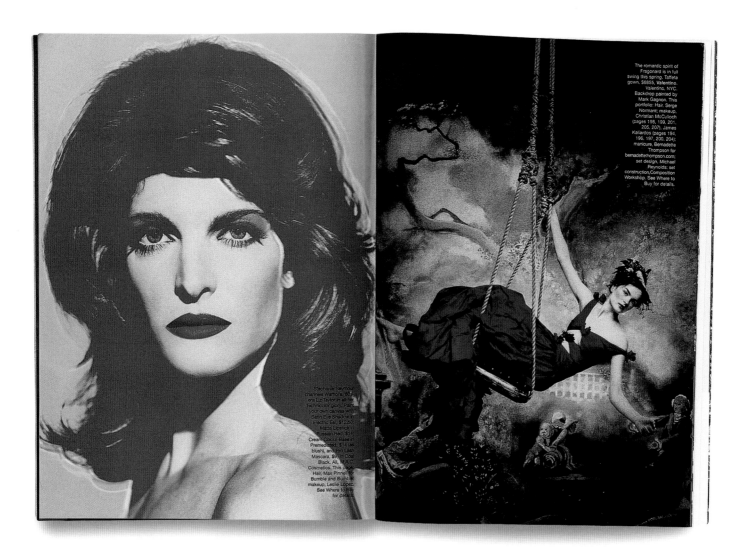

Stephanie Seymour channels Warhol's '60s-era Liz Taylor in all her Technicolor glory. Paint your own canvas with Satin Eye Shadow in Electric Eel, $12.50; Matte Lipstick in Russian Red, $14; Cream Colour Base in Premeditated, $14 (as blush), and Pro Lash Mascara, $9 in Coal Black. All, M.A.C. Cosmetics. This page: Hair, Max Pinnel for Bumble and Bumble; makeup, Leslie Lopez. See Where to Buy for details.

The romantic spirit of Fragonard is in full swing this spring. Taffeta gown, $6855, Valentino, Valentino, NYC. Backdrop painted by Mark Gagnon. This portfolio: Hair, Serge Normant; makeup, Christian McCulloch (pages 198, 199, 201, 205, 207), James Kaliardos (pages 194, 196, 197, 200, 204); manicure, Bernadette Thompson for bernadettethompson.com; set design, Michael Reynolds; set construction,Composition Workshop. See Where to Buy for details.

Rolling Stone

rollingstone.com
ISSUE 880 · OCTOBER 25, 2001 · $3.95

9.11.01

PHOTOGRAPH BY MARK SELIGER

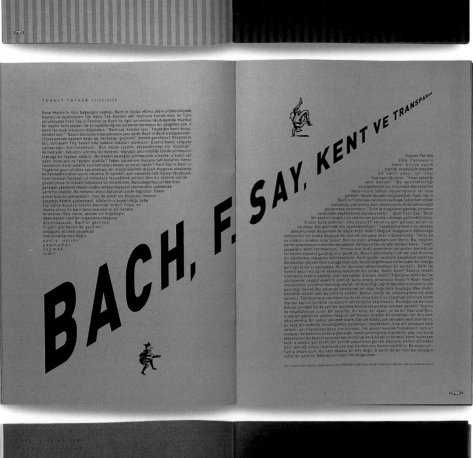

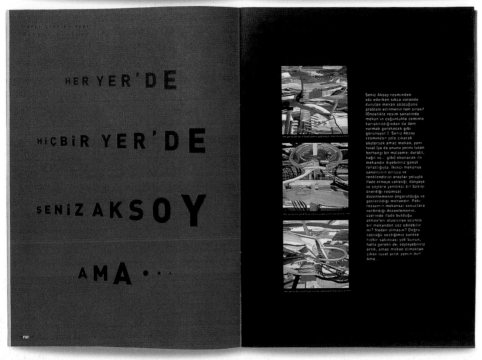

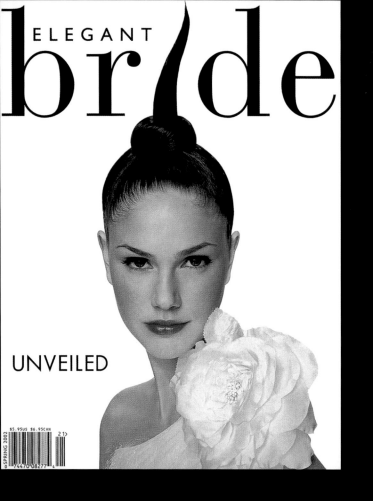

ELEGANT
br/de

UNVEILED

$5.95US $6.95CAN

SPRING 2002

0 74470 08277 4   2 1>

'Matador Magazine: **Volume E'** Design Firm: **Pentagram Design Ltd.** Art Director: **Fernando Gutierrez** Client: **La Fabrica**   Editorial **100,101**

(this spread) Design Firm: Sasaki Assoicates Art Director: John Barry Designers: John Barry, Brian Pearce, Jeff Sprague and Scott Love Photographers: Lucy Chen and Scott Love Client: Putnam Investments

NORTH CROSSING

CUMMINGS

EMERSON

North Entry

The Commons

The Marketplace

South Entry

DIRECTORY

(this spread) Design Firm: Sasaki Assoicates Art Director: John Barry Designers: John Barry, Brian Pearce, Jeff Sprague and Scott Love Photographers: Lucy Chen and Scott Love Client: Putnam Investments

BARTLETT

Design Firm: Sasaki Assoicates Art Director: John Barry Designers: John Barry, Brian Pearce, Jeff Sprague and Scott Love Photographers: Lucy Chen and Scott Love Client: Putnam Investments

Teknion

Design Firm: Vanderbyl Design Creative Director: Michael Vanderbyl Art Director: Michael Vanderbyl Designers: Michael Vanderbyl, Peter Fishel and Jeremy Regenbogen Client: Teknion Inc.

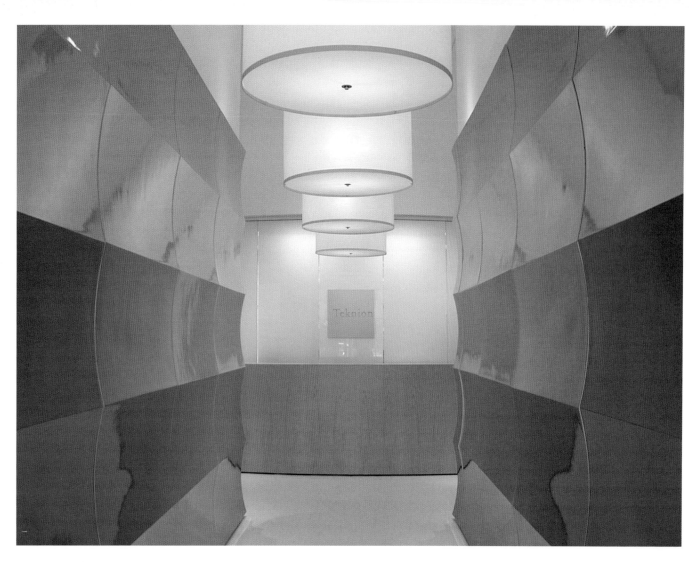

(this spread) Design Firm: Vanderbyl Design Creative Director: Michael Vanderbyl Art Director: Michael Vanderbyl Designers: Michael Vanderbyl, Peter Fishel and Jeremy Regenbogen Client: Teknion Inc.

(this spread) 'The British Galleries 1500-1900' Design Firm: Rose-Innes Associates Creative Directors: Crispin Rose-Innes and Grita Rose-Innes Art Directors: Crispin Rose-Innes and Grita Rose-Innes Designers: Crispin Rose-Innes and Grita Rose-Innes Client: Victoria

GALLERY 125c

INFLUENCES FROM OTHER CULTURES

TRAINING FOR DESIGNERS

GALLERY
123

British Galleries
1760–1900
LEVEL 4

WHO LED TASTE?

The National Gallery
of British Art at
South Kensington

WHO LED TASTE?

Henry Cole and the
Founders of the V&A

The National Gallery
of British Art at
the South Kensington
Museum

1857

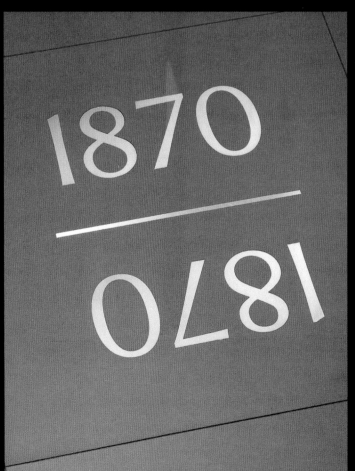

1870

1870

(this spread) 'Pure Beauty' Design Firm: Pentagram Design., Ltd. Art Director: Lorenzo Apicella Design Assistants: Johanna Molineus and: Zlatko Haban Client: Boots

'Ceramic Tiles of Italy A.I.A. Exhibit' Design Firm: Mauk Design Art Director: Mitchell Mauk Designer: Ingrid Ballmann Photographer: Andy Caulfield Client: Italian Trade Commission

"Wirlankarra yanama.
Yurlu nyinku mirda yurndarirda."

"Go with a clear, open and accepting spirit,
and the country will not treat you badly."

(this spread) 'Karijini Visitor Centre' Design Firm: David Lancashire Design Creative Director: David Lancashire Designers: Heidi Stoll and Tony Gilevski Copywriters: David Webster and Di Lancashire Client: Department of Conservation and Land Management

'There was a time when we would all get together at a ceremony. Maybe a new baby would be taken there and everybody would say. 'Eh, what's this baby, where was it born?' Then the mother and father would say, 'He was born at that place.' Everybody would say. "Oh, that's his country, we all know his country."'

SLIM PARKER
MARTIDJA BANYJIMA LANGUAGE GROUP

Karijini National Park is a landscape full of the memories of relations and ancestors. The country is marked everywhere by the birthplaces and burial sites of mothers and fathers, grandmothers and grandfathers, aunties and uncles, brothers and sisters.

Rodney Parker (son of Wobby Parker), Wobby Parker and Patrick Long (a richero) and Eric Carey (grandson of Wobby through kinship), at Wobby Parker's birthplace.

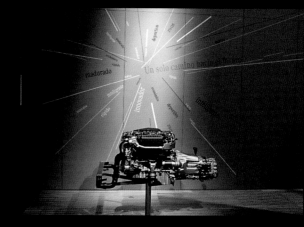

Mercedes Benz & Smart at the Automotive Show in Barcelona 2001¹ Design Firm: Design Roch Drei Creative Director: Susanne Wacker Art Director: Susanne Wacker Designer: Jörg Dengler Photographer: Andreas Keller Architect: Burling Schindler C

vida

descanso

emoción

espacio

tiempo

vivir los sueños

flotar, disfrutar, conducir, soñar

subir, salir, descubrir,

C 220 CDI

Caixas são Escritas íntimas   Desenhos antigos Tampas fechadas

'Take Three' Design Firm: Mirko Ilic Corp. Art Director: Minh Uong Illustrator: Mirko Ilic Client: Village Voice

Illustration 124,125

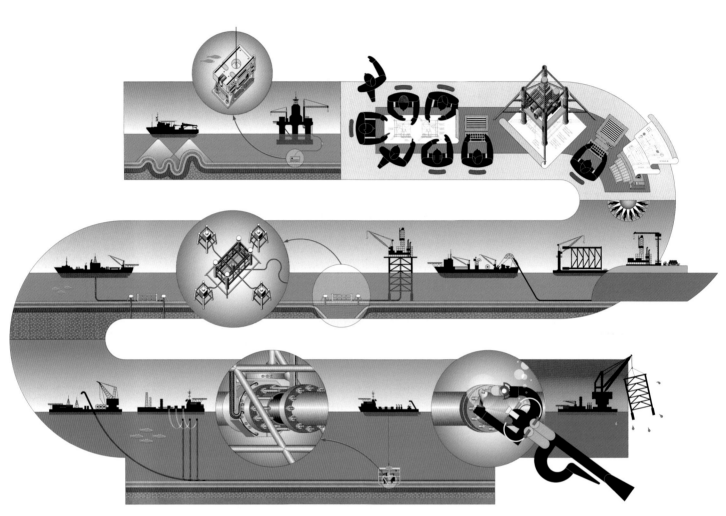

'How Stolt Works' Design Firm: CGI Brandsense Creative Director: Simon Shaw Art Director: Sue Purkiss-Webb Illustrator: Tilly Northedge Client: Stolt Offshore

Christina Ullman Designer: Christina Ullman Illustrator: Christina Ullman (this page) 'Steering Wheel' Design Firm: Vitro Robertson Art Director: Marc Chila Illustrator: Peter Krämer Client: Yamaha   Illustration 128, 129

(Opposite)'The Kiss' Design Firm: Chirstina Ullman Design Creative Director: Christina Ullman Art Director:

'Vision Icons' Design Firm: T. G. Madison Advertising Creative Director: Virgil Shutze Art Director: Kerry Hadaway Illustrator: Mike Kasun Client: Metlife

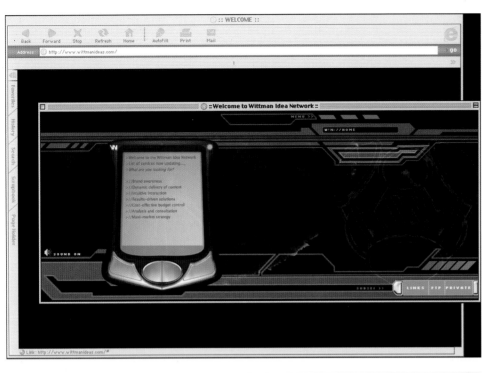

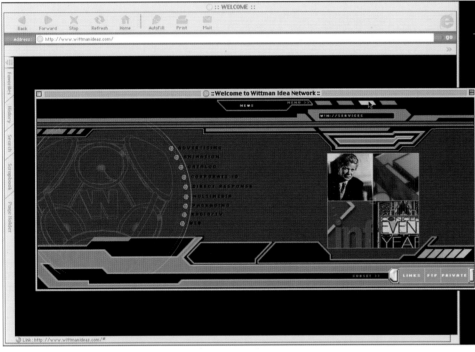

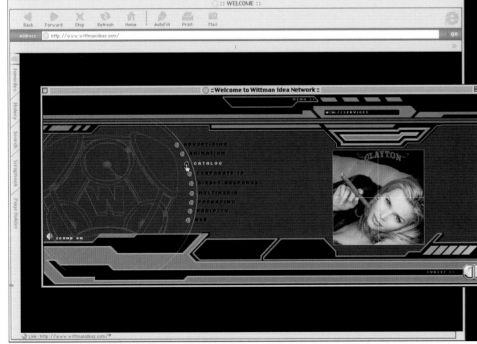

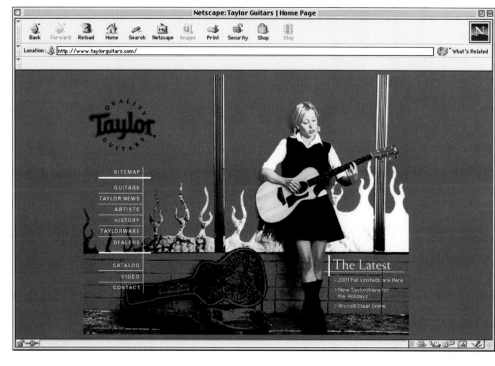

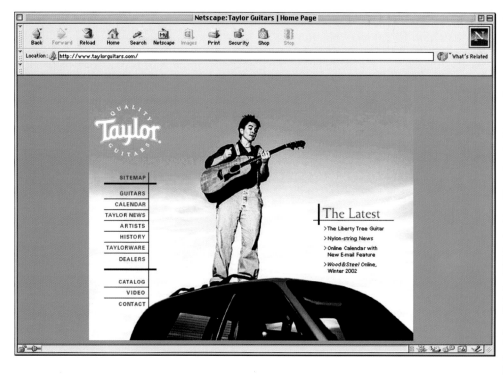

'Taylor Guitars Website 2001' Design Firm: Mires Creative Director: Scott Mires Art Director: Scott Mires Designer: Gale Spitzley Photographer: Marshall Harrington Programming: Sam Grogan Client: Taylor Guitars   Interactive **132, 133**

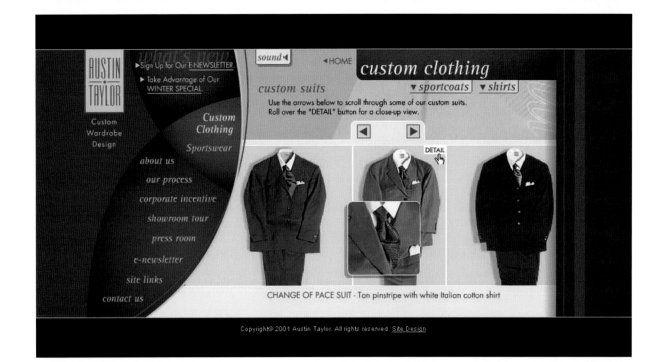

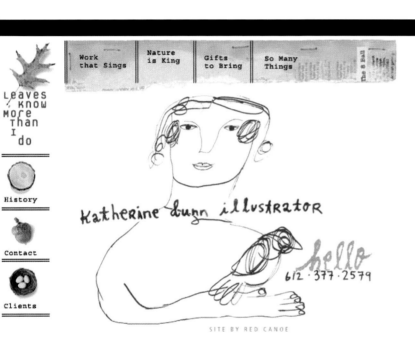

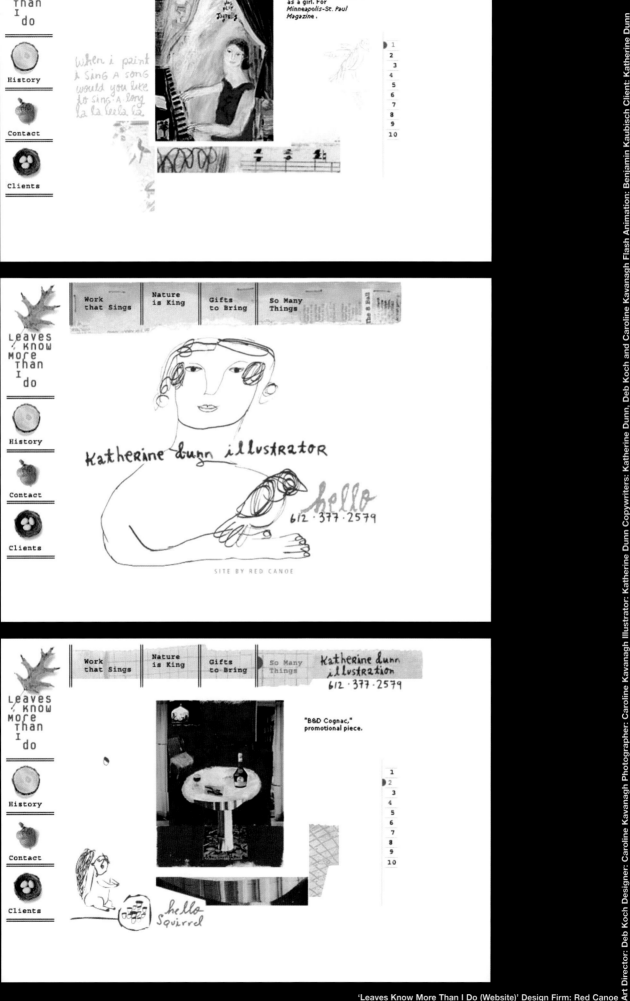

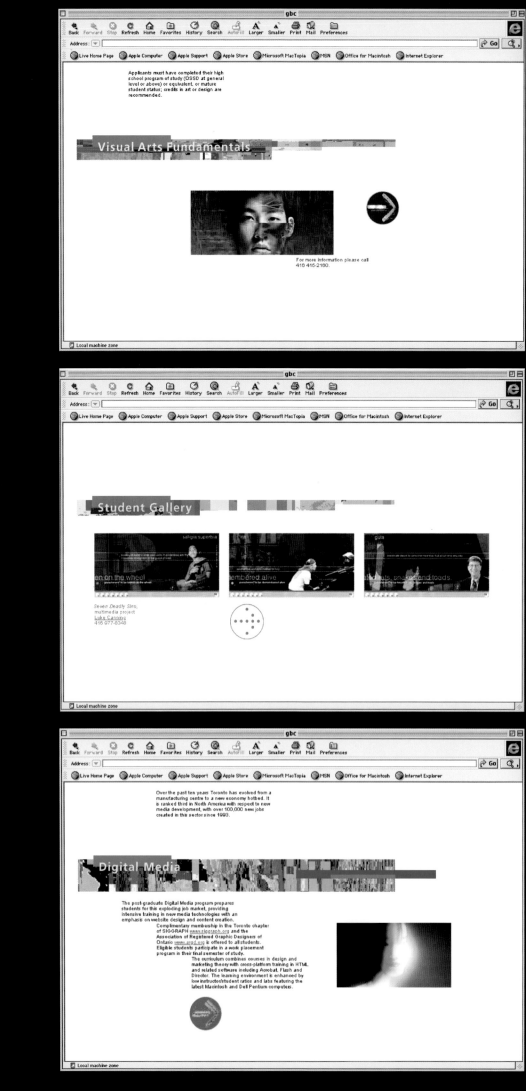

Applicants must have completed their high
school program of study (OSSD at general
level or above) or equivalent, or mature
student status; credits in art or design are
recommended.

Visual Arts Fundamentals

For more information please call
416 415-2180.

Student Gallery

Seven Deadly Sins;
multimedia project
Luke Canning
416 977-8348

Over the past ten years Toronto has evolved from a
manufacturing centre to a new economy hotbed. It
is ranked third in North America with respect to new
media development, with over 100,000 new jobs
created in this sector since 1993.

Digital Media

The post-graduate Digital Media program prepares
students for this exploding job market, providing
intensive training in new media technologies with an
emphasis on website design and content creation.

Complimentary membership in the Toronto chapter
of SIGGRAPH www.siggraph.org and the
Association of Registered Graphic Designers of
Ontario www.argd.org is offered to all students.
Eligible students participate in a work placement
program in their final semester of study.

The curriculum combines courses in design and
marketing theory with cross-platform training in HTML
and related software including Acrobat, Flash and
Director. The learning environment is enhanced by
low instructor/student ratios and labs featuring the
latest Macintosh and Dell Pentium computers.

dumb box productions

◄ BACK TO MAIN PAGE

Factory & Process

1	2	3	4	5
6	7	8	9	10
11	12	13	14	15
16	17	18	19	20
21	22	23	24	25
26	27	28	29	30
31	32	33	34	35
36	37	38	39	40
41	42	43	44	45
46	47	48	49	50
51	52	53	54	55

---

dumb box productions

FEATURES

NEW PRODUCTS
NY SHOWROOM
LA SHOWROOM
DESIGN STUDIO
ARCHITECTURE
INTERIOR DESIGN
FACTORY & PROCESS
PRESS (COMING SOON)
INSTALLATIONS (COMING SOON)
dumbbox SUPPORTS

○ CABINETS ○ COCKTAIL TABLES ○ BEDS ○ CONSOLES ○ DESKS ○ DINING TABLES ○ LOUNGE SEATING ○ PULL-UP SEATING ○ SIDE TABLES ○ MIRRORS

---

dumb box productions

◄ BACK TO MAIN PAGE

Featured Architects

SCROLL ▼

1100 Architect
&derson Architects
Alex Gorlin
Agrest & Gandelsonas
ARO
Bromley Caldari
David Ling Architects
Escher GuneWardena
Fox & Fowle Architects
Gabellini
Hariri & Hariri , Inc.
kOnyk
Krueck • Sexton
Kuth Ranieri
Lewis.Tsurumaki.Lewis
Mesh
nArchitects

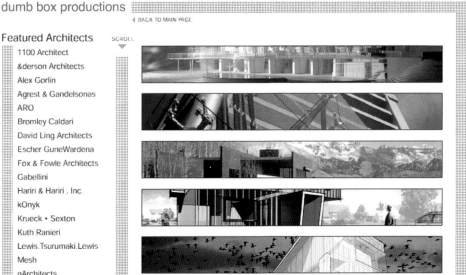

House of Horrors' Design Firm: DNA Design Ltd. Creative Director: Grenville Main Designers: Sarah Long, Steve le Marguand, Matthew Barnes and Angela Lord Photographer: Matthew Barnes Illustrator: Dean Proudfoot Client: Lorraine Carryer Interactive 138,139

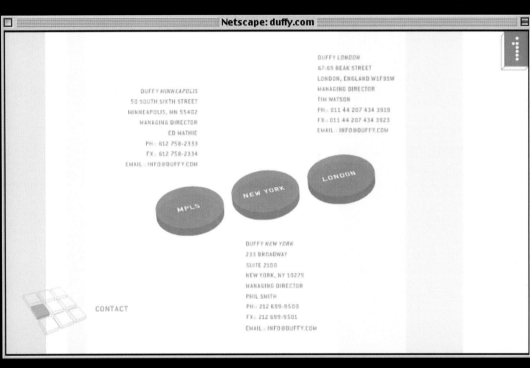

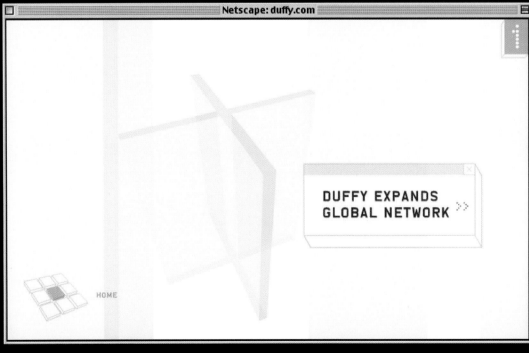

www.malcolmtarlofsky.com Design Firm: Red Canoe Art Director: Deb Koch Designer: Caroline Kavanagh Illustrator: Malcolm Tarlofsky Copywriters: Malcolm Tarlofsky and Deb Koch Flash Scripting: Benjamin Kaubisch Client: Malcolm Tarlofsky

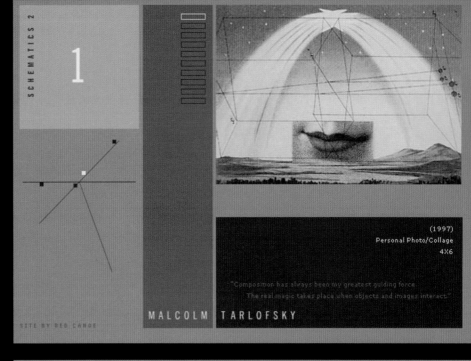

SCHEMATICS 2

1

(1997)
Personal Photo/Collage
4X6

"Composition has always been my greatest guiding force.
The real magic takes place when objects and images interact."

MALCOLM TARLOFSKY

SITE BY RED CANOE

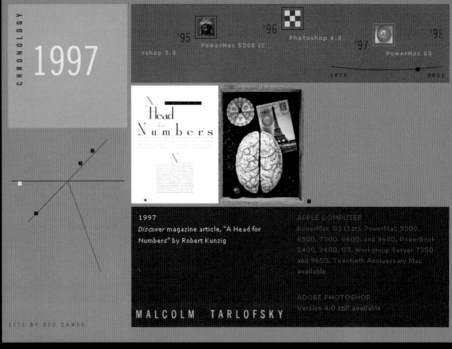

CHRONOLOGY

1997

'95 '96 '97 '98
oshop 3.0 PowerMac 5200 LC Photoshop 4.0 PowerMac G3

1975 2001

1997
Discover magazine article, "A Head for
Numbers" by Robert Kunzig

APPLE COMPUTER
PowerMac G3 (1st), PowerMac 5500,
6500, 7300, 8600, and 9600, PowerBook
2400, 3400, G3, Workgroup Server 7350
and 9650, Twentieth Anniversary Mac
available

ADOBE PHOTOSHOP
Version 4.0 still available

MALCOLM TARLOFSKY

SITE BY RED CANOE

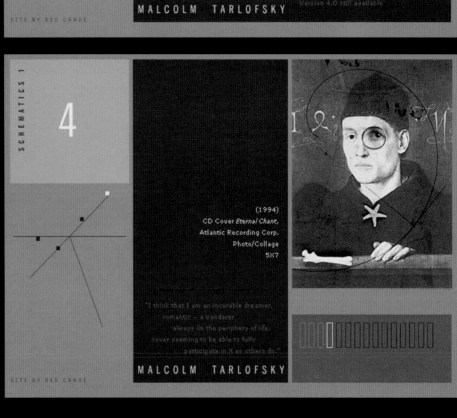

SCHEMATICS 1

4

(1994)
CD Cover *Eternal Chant,*
Atlantic Recording Corp.
Photo/Collage
5X7

"I think that I am an incurable dreamer,
romantic – a wanderer
always on the periphery of life,
never seeming to be able to fully
participate in it as others do."

MALCOLM TARLOFSKY

SITE BY RED CANOE

Design Firm: Savas Cekic Design Studio Creative Director: Savas Cekic Art Director: Savas Cekic Designer: Savas Cekic Client: Doga Yayinevi

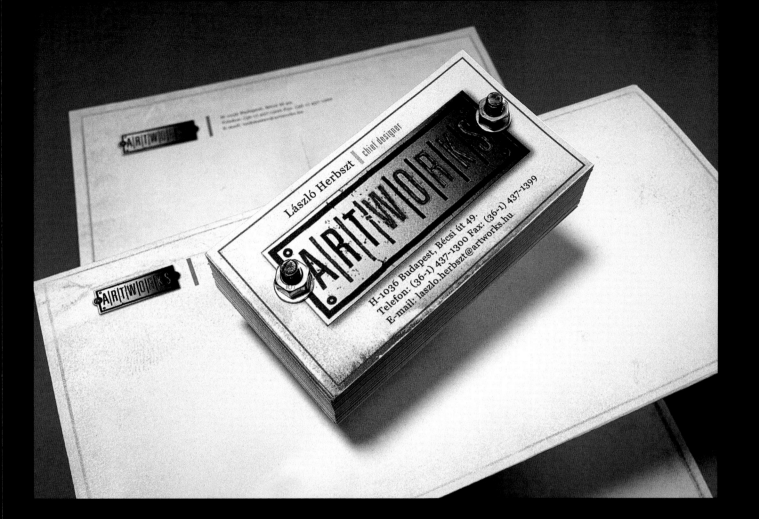

László Herbszt | chief designer

AIRITIWIOIRIKIS

H-1036 Budapest, Bécsi út 49.
Telefon: (36-1) 437-1300 Fax: (36-1) 437-1399
E-mail: laszlo.herbszt@artworks.hu

stones
the printers

stones
the printers

Simon Hunt
Managing Director

Telephone 01295 252211
Facsimile 01295 273150
mobile 07909 687650
shunt@stonestheprinters.co.uk

with compliments

stones
the printers

Stones the Printers Limited
Unit 10, Acre Estate, Wildmere Road, Banbury, Oxon OX16 3ES
Telephone 01295 252211 Facsimile 01295 273150
ISDN 01295 701100 www.stonestheprinters.co.uk

Stones the Printers Limited
Unit 10, Acre Estate, Wildmere Road, Banbury, Oxon OX16 3ES Telephone 01295 252211 Facsimile 01295 273150
ISDN 01295 701100 www.stonestheprinters.co.uk

(this spread) Design Firm: DNA Design Ltd. Creative Director: Grenville Main Art Director: Charlie Ward Designer: Charlie Ward Photographer: Andy Radka Illustrator: Charlie Ward Copywriter: Charlie Ward Client: Above Ground Level

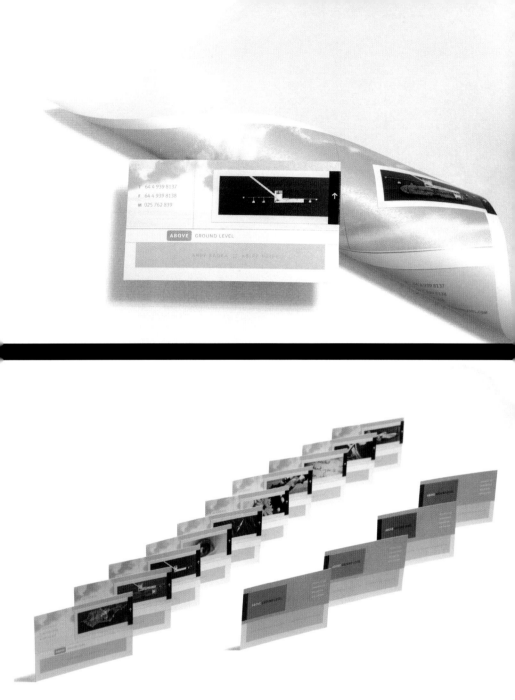

LANDCRAFTERS

Design Firm: i.design Designer: Jonathan Ingram Client: Landcrafters (opposite from top, 1) Design Firm: RBMM Designer: Dan Birlew Client: Starr Contractors (2) Design Firm: [b] studios Art Director: Brandi C. Lariscy Designer: Brandi C. Lariscy Photographer: Brandi C. Lariscy Client: Charlotte Ad Club (3) Design Firm: Mark Oliver, Inc. (4) Design Firm: Kilmer & Kilmer Creative Director: Richard Kilmer Client: Vandyke Software (5) Design Firm: Savas Cekic Design Studio Creative Director: Savas Cekic Art Director: Savas Cekic Designer: Savas Cekic Client: Doga Yayinevi

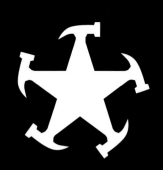

CHARLOTTE AD CLUB

gary pools

(from top, 1) 'Summer Theatre Fesitval' Design Firm: Kellum McClain Inc. Designer: Ron Kellum Client: The Actors Ensemble (2) Design Firm: Myra Nowlin Art Director: Myra Nowlin Designer: Myra J. Nowlin Client: Wiley Publishing Company (3) Design Firm: Bradford Lawton Design Group, Inc. Creative Director: Bradford Lawton Designers: Becky Hahs and Bradford Lawton Client: Gary Pools (4) Design Firm: Myra Nowlin Art Director: Myra J. Nowlin Designer: Myra J. Nowlin Client: Skate 2000 (5) Design Firm: Sibley/Peteet Design Creative Director: Tim McClure Art Director: Rex Peteet Designer: Rex Peteet Illustrator: Rex Peteet Client: McClure Gourmet

Design Firm: Cid Lab

(from top, 1) Design Firm: RBMM Designer: Jacob Ristau Illustrator: Jacob Ristau Client: Tri-Pisces (2) Design Firm: Planet Propaganda Creative Director: Dana Lytle Designer: Brad DeMarea Client: Wisconsin Film Festival (3) Design Firm: Laughlin/Constable - Griffin Design Creative Director: Jay Harris Client: Buell Motorcycle Company (4) Design Firm: RBMM Creative Director: Tom Nynas Art Director: Tom Nynas Designer: Tom Nynas Illustrator: Tom Nynas Client: RBMM (5) Design Firm: Wallace Church, Inc. Creative Director: Stan Church Art Director: Wendy Church Designer: Wendy Church Illustrator: Lucian Toma Client: Headline Productions

Design Firm: Sparc, Inc. Creative Director: Richard Cassis Art Director: Richard Cassis Designer: Richard Cassis Illustrator: Richard Cassis Client: Sue Blattner, Landscape Design

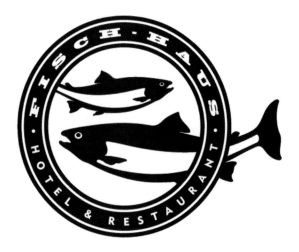

Creative Director: Tim McClure Art Directors: Rex Peteet and Matt Heck Designer: David Guillory Illustrator: David Guillory Client: Lajitar (3) Design Firm: Newton.Ehb Creative Director: Graham Walker Designer: Graham Walker Client: Freeform

(from top, 1, 2, 4, 5) Design Firm: Sibley/Peteet Design

Design Firm: Artworks Designer: László Herbszt Client: Artworks

Design Firm: IE Design, Los Angeles Creative Director: Marcie Carson Art Director: Marcie Carson Designers: Marcie Carson and Cya Nelson Client: MGM Grand, Pearl Restaurant

Design Firm: Graphics & Designing, Inc.

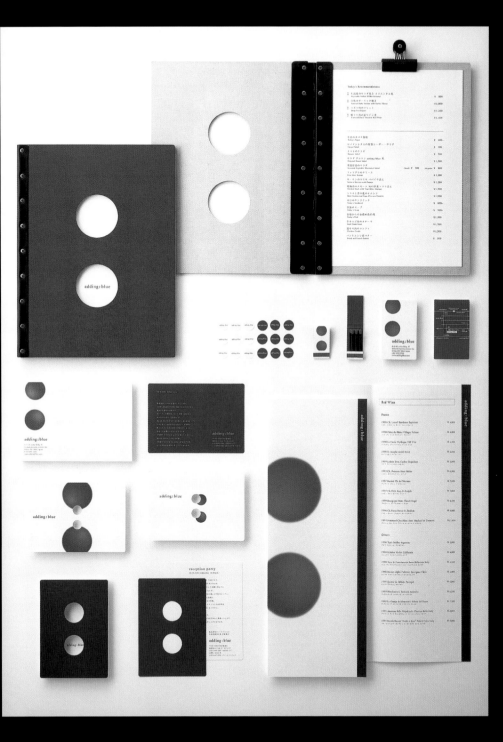

LOS BELKING'S · LOS DOLTON'S · LOS SILVERTON'S · WE ALL TOGETHER · RÍO · DANAI & PATEANDO LATAS · ARENA HASH · LA BANDA AZUL · DUDÓ · NOSEQUIÉN Y LOS NOSECUANTOS IVONNE Y LOS MERCANTILES · LOS ZOPILOTES · PATRICIO SUÁREZ VÉRTIZ · CHRISTIAN MEIER ▶

CRONICA DEL ROCK PERUANO

[POP ROCK] CD2

LOS YORK'S · LOS SHAIN'S · THE (ST. THOMAS) PEPPER SMELTER · TRAFFIC SOUND · FRÁGIL MIKI GONZÁLEZ · JAS · MAR DE COPAS · LA LIGA DEL SUEÑO · DOLORES DELIRIO · RAFO RÁEZ CEMENTERIO CLUB · ELECTRO Z · ÍNDIGO ▶▶▶▶▶▶▶▶▶▶▶▶▶▶▶▶▶▶▶▶▶▶▶▶▶▶▶

CRONICA DEL ROCK PERUANO

[MODERN ROCK] CD1

TELEGRAPH AVENUE · GERARDO MANUEL Y EL HUMO · EL POLEN · EL OPIO · FRÁGIL · DEL PUEBLO Y DEL BARRIO · MIKI GONZÁLEZ · TIERRA SUR · TURMANYÉ · LOS MOJARRAS PSICOSIS · LA SARITA · D'MENTE COMÚN · UNIDAD CENTRAL ▶▶▶▶▶▶▶▶▶▶▶▶▶▶▶▶

CRONICA DEL ROCK PERUANO

[ROCK ALTERNATIVO] CD4

LOS SAICOS · LAGHONIA · PAX · TARKUS · NARCOSIS · LEUSEMIA · M.A.S.A.C.R.E. · G-3 · VOZ PROPIA · RADIO CRIMINAL · EL AIRE · METADONA · AVISPÓN VERDE · AEROPAJITAS ▶▶▶▶▶ ▶▶

CRONICA DEL ROCK PERUANO

[ROCK ALTERNATIVO] CD3

Designers: Xavier Conesa and Veruzka Noriega Copywriters: Francisco Hernandez and Pedro Conejo Design Editor: Claudia Burga-Cisneros Photography Editor: Ana Cecilia Gonzales-Vigil Client: El Comercio

'Cronica del Rock Peruano — The History of Peruvian Rock Music' Design Firm: El Comercio Art Director: Xavier Conesa

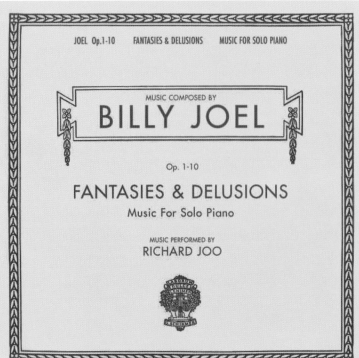

JOEL Op.1-10   FANTASIES & DELUSIONS   MUSIC FOR SOLO PIANO

MUSIC COMPOSED BY
BILLY JOEL

Op. 1-10

FANTASIES & DELUSIONS
Music For Solo Piano

MUSIC PERFORMED BY
RICHARD JOO

Tantric
YOU I'D BE TRYING TO CHANGE MYSELF CHORUS PARANOID... YOU ALL ALONE THERE IN THE DARK SHADOWS
I MOVE I'M TIED UP HERE HE SAID I'VE SEEN THIS PAIN BEFORE SOMETIMES I WANT TO DISAPPEAR
NOISE INSIDE
WE'LL SEE THAT YOU AND ME WILL FINALLY BREATHE AGAIN HOW CAN I LIVE IN THE PAST NOW

Designer: Hans Seeger Photographer: Richard Burbridge Client: Aesthetics

Design Firm: VSA Partners, Inc. Art Director: Hans Seeger Designer: Hans Seeger Photographer: Richard Burbridge Client: Aesthetics

Designers: David Harlan and Kim Biggs Photographer: Dennis Keely Client: Maverick Recording Co. (bottom) Design Firm: VSA Partners, Inc. Art Director: Hans Seeger Designer: Hans Seeger Photographer: Richard Burbridge Client: Aesthetics

(top) 'Tantric (Self-Titled)' Design Firm: Popglory Creative Directors: Kim Biggs and David Harlan Art Directors: Kim Biggs and David Harlan

'Fusebox' Design Firm: Th Creative Director: Scott McDaniel Designers: Clark Hook and Blake Tannery Client: Forefront Records   Music 172,173

Se staden:

2001
Arkitekturåret
www.arkitekturmuseet.se

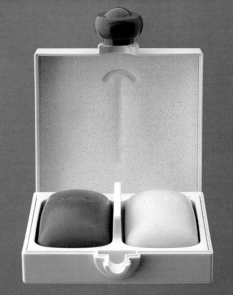

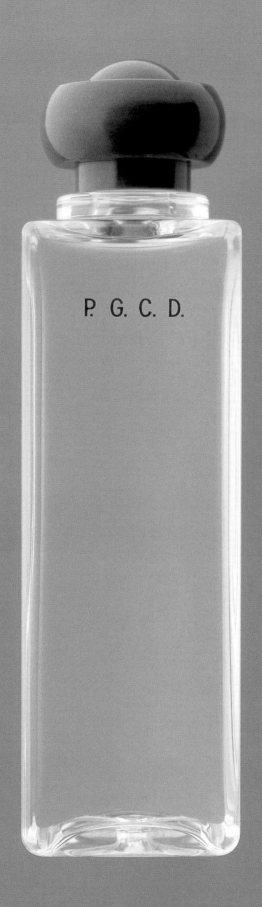

(this spread) 'Guest & Me' Design Firm: Taku Satoh Design Office, Inc. Art Director: Taku Satoh Designers: Taku Satoh and Shino Misawa Client: Lion Corporation

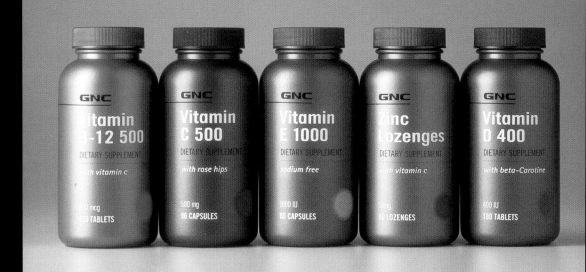

Design Firm: Nike Inc. Creative Director: Byron Jacobs Art Director: Byron Jacobs Designer: Janet Boye Photographer: Marcus Swanson Client: Nike Eyeware

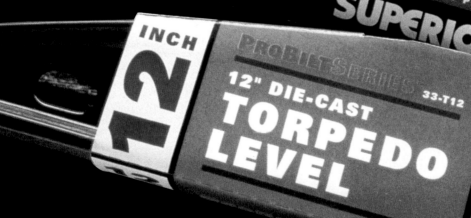

Packaging **182, 183**

and Dean Zillwood Illustrator: Phillipa Devenport Copywriter: Andrew Gair Client: Telecom New Zealand

Design Firm: DNA Design Ltd. Creative Director: Grenville Main Art Director: Charlie Ward Designers: Charlie Ward and Sarah Laing Photographers: Jono Rotman

(this spread) Design Firm: Fossil Creative Director: Tim Hale Art Director: Stephen Zhang Designer: Dominique Pierron Client: Fossil

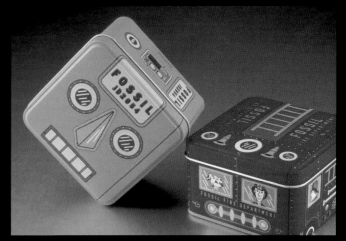

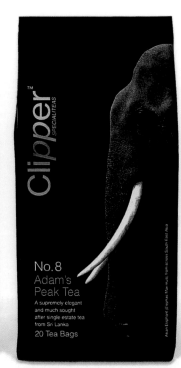

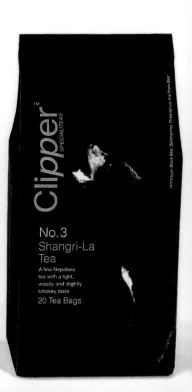

'Stack Tins' Design Firm: Sandstrom Design Creative Director: Steve Sandstrom Art Director: Steve Sandstrom Designer: Steve Sandstrom Copywriters: Steve Sandoz and Palmer Pettersen Production Designer: Sarah Cook Client: Tazo Packaging 186,187

Awake™
FULL LEAF BLACK TEA
FEUILLES DE THÉ NOIR
A breakfast tea of character,
invigorating any time of day.

FULL
LEAF

BLACK TEA T-80005

Net Wt / Poids Net 28g (1oz)

Calm™
HERBAL INFUSION
TISANE D'HERBAGE
An exotic, relaxing blend
of whole flowers and fragrant
cut and sorted botanicals.

CUT &
SORTED

HERBAL INFUSION T-80110

Net Wt / Poids Net 10g (.35oz)

Zen™
FULL
LEAF

Awake™
FULL LEAF BLACK TEA
FEUILLES DE THÉ NOIR
A breakfast tea of character,
invigorating any time of day.

BLACK TEA

Net Wt / Poids Net 28g (1oz)

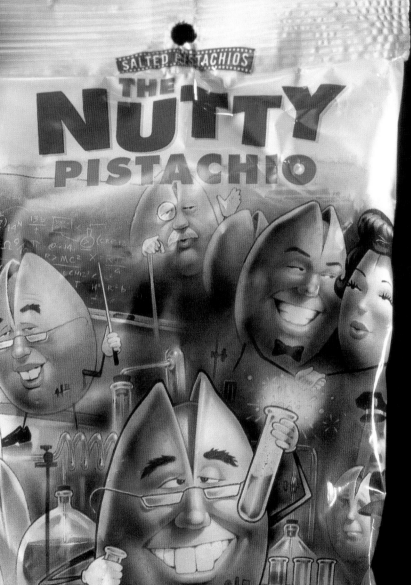

'Reebok Fitness Water' Design Firm: Karacters Design Group Creative Director: Maria Kennedy Art Director: Matthew Clark Designer: Matthew Clark Client: Clearly Canadian Beverage Corp.

(top left) Design Firm: Gollings Pidgeon Creative Director: David Pidgeon Designers: David Pidgeon and Marianna Tsvilin Client: Di Stasio Wines (top right) Design Firm: Pentagram Design, Ltd. Art Director: Fernando Gutierrez Creative Director: Deshesa Gago and Altos de Lanzaga' Design Firm: Pentagram Design, Ltd. Art Director: Fernando Gutierrez
Design Assistant: Marc Catala Client: Telmo Rodriguez (bottom left) 'Worshippers and Crow Flies' Design Firm: Scooter Design Creative Directors: Chris Williams and James Francis Art Director: Chris Williams Designer: Chris Williams Photographer: Ross Brown
Design Firm: Design Bridge Ltd. Creative Director: Graham Shearsby Designer: Huiwen Chan Client: Prats & Symington Lda
Copywriter: James Francis Client: Hidden Valley Vineyard (bottom right) 'Chryseia' Design Firm: Design Bridge Ltd. Creative Director: Graham Shearsby Designer: Huiwen Chan Client: Prats & Symington Lda

'Sandeman 40 Year Old Port' Design Firm: Wren & Rowe Ltd. Creative Director: Michael Rowe Designer: Emma Colwell Hand Lettering: Bob Stradling Client: Sandeman & Co.   Packaging 194,195

(this spread) 'Potlatch Peak Magazine' Design Firm: Louey/Rubino Design Group Creative Directors: Robert Louey and Karen Dacus Designer: Robert Louey Concept/Content: Karen Dacus Client: Potlach Corporation

UP

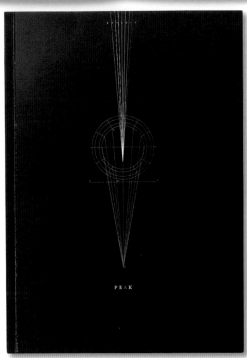

PEAK

TORRENT OF LIGHT AND RIVER OF AIR, ALONG WHOSE BED THE GLIMMERING STARS ARE SEEN, LIKE GOLD AND SILVER SANDS IN SOME RAVINE...

HENRY WADSWORTH LONGFELLOW, AMERICAN POET

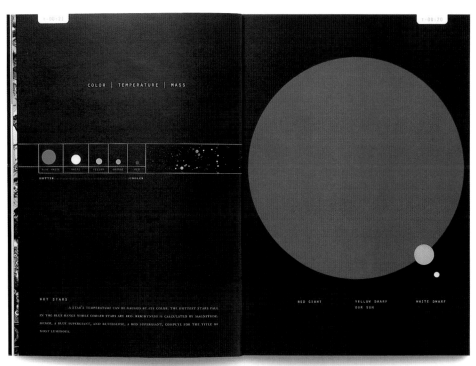

COLOR | TEMPERATURE | MASS

HOTTER..................................COOLER

RED GIANT   YELLOW DWARF   WHITE DWARF
                OUR SUN

HOT STARS
       A STAR'S TEMPERATURE CAN BE GAUGED BY ITS COLOR. THE HOTTEST STARS FALL
IN THE BLUE RANGE WHILE COOLER STARS ARE RED. BRIGHTNESS IS CALCULATED BY MAGNITUDE.
DENEB, A BLUE SUPERGIANT, AND BETELGEUSE, A RED SUPERGIANT, COMPETE FOR THE TITLE OF
MOST LUMINOUS.

W.M. KECK OBSERVATORY AT MAUNA KEA, HAWAII

MARS VIKING LANDER: 1976

LANDER 1   SOL 556   LANDER 1   SOL 688

"THE CHANCES AGAINST ANYTHING

MAN-LIKE ON MARS ARE A MILLION TO ONE"

WAR OF THE WORLDS, H.G. WELLS

A green banana is as good
as a yellow banana.
But only on Phoeno is it a
real good banana.
frei zitiert nach André Breton, Bananenmanifest

Bananen/Bananas

2–**15**
für
Stück **Pfg.**

Phoeno!
Eine Marke von Scheufelen

Oh, the delicious fruits that we have here and in Syria!
Orange gardens miles in extent, citrons, pomegranates;
but the most delicious thing after Phoeno is a banana.
frei zitiert nach Benjamin Disraeli (1804 – 1881), Britischer Premierminister

(this spread) 'Bananas' Design Firm: Scheufele Kommunikations-Agentur Creative Director: Beate Scheufele Copywriter: Wulf Goebel Client: Papierfabrik Scheufelen

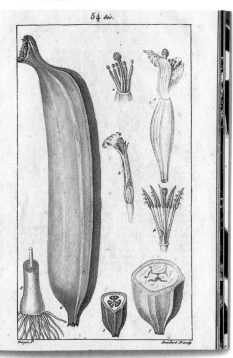

surface

superior <color fidelity>

Unbelievably vibrant, realistic color. Red that is truly red. Black with the intensity of jet. Skin tones that look real enough to touch. Ikono faithfully replicates the colors of your original photo. It's able to do this because of its super-smooth surface—a surface that allows uniform reflection of light. Uneven surfaces cause light to scatter, graying and dulling the image. But Ikono's smooth surface minimizes light interference, giving you true-to-life color on the printed page.

exceptional <ink gloss>

minimal <dot gain>

You can drop all concerns about dot gain when you're printing on Ikono. Ikono's super-smooth surface ensures that ink dries on the paper surface. The result? Sharp, clear dots that hold their size and shape. With Ikono, you won't get any fuzzy-edged dots... they'll all have beautifully crisp edges. With Ikono, you won't get mottled images. In fact, with Ikono, what you will get is a sharp, clear image. You can't ask for more than that!

Ikono's super-smooth surface and high gloss finish produce a dazzling combination that gives you bright, shiny ink gloss on page after page, image after image. That's because ink can't seep into the body of the paper. It stays right on the surface, where its true sheen adds to the beauty of the printed image. You can depend on Ikono to give you results that command attention. After all, Ikono is simply the best.

excellent

<print contrast>

When you think of print contrast, what do you envision? The contrast between saturated colors? The contrast between printed image and unprinted paper? The contrast between highlights and shadows? You get them all with Ikono. No other paper can compare with Ikono when it comes to contrast—because Ikono's super-smooth surface, exceptional whiteness, high brightness and superior gloss make the difference. You'll see that difference on every page of this book.

(this spread) 'Kekkai' Design Firm: Kokokumaru Inc. Art Director: Yoshimaru Takahashi Designer: Yoshimaru Takahashi Client: Oji Paper Co. Ltd.

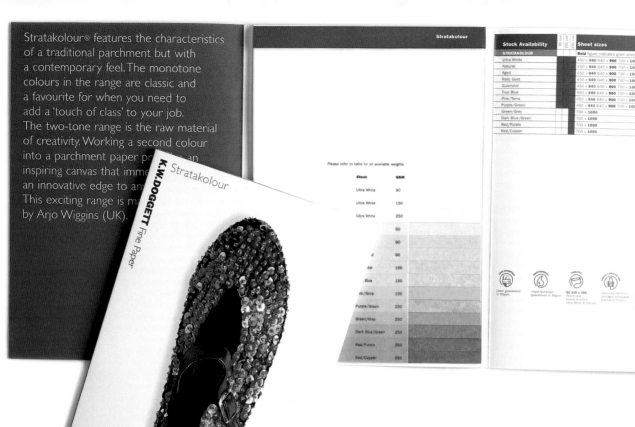

Stratakolour® features the characteristics of a traditional parchment but with a contemporary feel. The monotone colours in the range are classic and a favourite for when you need to add a 'touch of class' to your job. The two-tone range is the raw material of creativity. Working a second colour into a parchment paper pr[...] an inspiring canvas that imme[...] an innovative edge to an[...] This exciting range is ma[...] by Arjo Wiggins (UK).

Fine Paper

K.W.DOGGETT Medley Satin A1 & Satin Clear
Fine Paper

K.W.DOGGETT Paradox - Dual Finish
Fine Paper

K.W.DOGGETT

essebo Design

K.W.DOGGETT OCM Original & New
Fine Paper

K.W.DOGGETT Lustrulux & Finess
Fine Paper

K.W.DOGGETT Countryside
Fine Paper

PP Synthetic

nooth

K.W.DOGGETT Laser-Tec, High Tech & Reflex Laser
Fine Paper

Kaskad

kolour

K.W.DOGGETT Cambric / Enhance / Ridge - Embossed
Fine Paper

K.W.DOGGETT RSVP - True Felt
Fine Paper

EN BUSCA DE LA BELLEZA EN EL MUNDO

En busca de la belleza en el mundo
Encuentros esenciales

Tercera edición del concurso
de diseño de escaparates Hermès
Inscripción:
hasta el 15 de febrero de 2001
Entrega de proyectos:
hasta el 27 de abril de 2001 a las 15:00h
Organización y Secretaría Técnica:
BCD, Barcelona Centro de Diseño
Av. Diagonal 452
08006 Barcelona

HERMÈS

'Issey Miyake Insetto' Design Firm: Taku Satoh Design Office Inc. Art Director: Taku Satoh Designer: Taku Satoh Photographer: Yukio Shimizu Client: SFJ, Inc.

MITSUI & CO., LTD.

Ojitex (Vietnam) Co., Ltd.

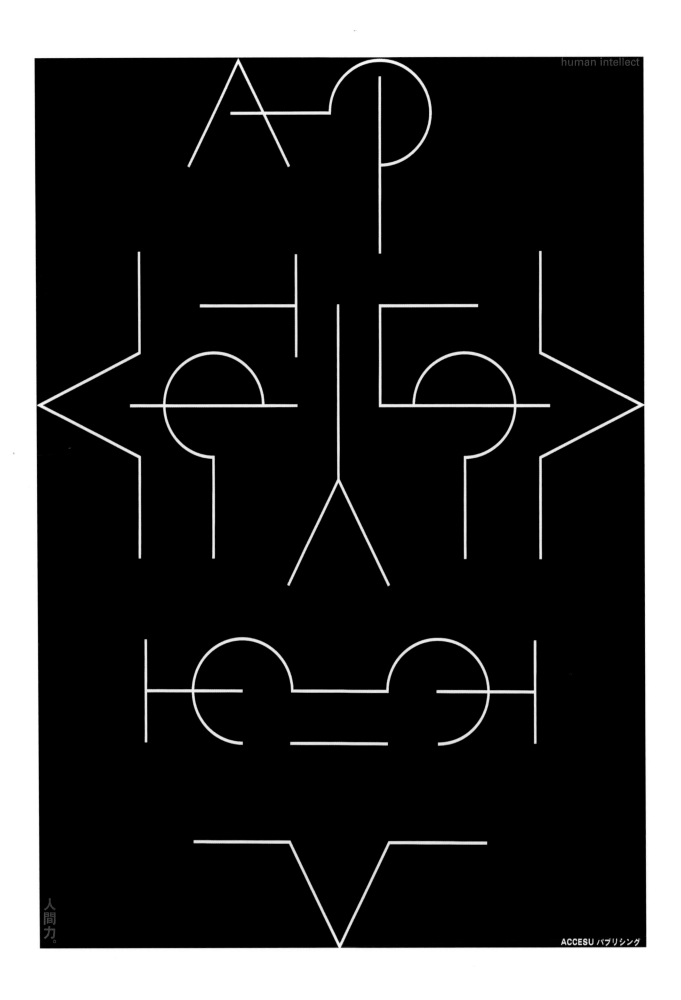

'AP' Design Firm: Akio Okumura Art Director: Akio Okumura Designer: Sae Nagaoka Client: Access Publishing

人間力。

ACCESU パブリシング

'Letter' Design Firm: Akio Okumura Art Director: Akio Okumura Designer: Yasuyo Fukamoto Client: Font 100

THE LAND OF THE FREE AND THE HOME OF THE BRAVE IN MEMORY OF THOSE WHO DIED SEPTEMBER 2001

Design Firm: Sayles Graphic Design Creative Director: John Sayles Art Director: John Sayles Designers: John Sayles and Som Inthalangsy Illustrator: John Sayles Copywriter: Annie Meacham Client: Art Fights Back

'Festival do Rio Trophy' Design Firm: Vinte Zero Um Creative Director: Jair de Souza Art Director: Jair de Souza Designers: Jair de Souza and Clara Martins Photographer: Philipe Meyer Client: Cima

ALTECLANSING

CENTER   SURROUND   VOLUME

'Mina 251' Design Firm: Macey Noyes Associates Creative Director: Tod Dawson Designers: Lenny Dichiara, Victor Ivenitsky and Giovanni Pagnotta Client: Altec Lansing

Ivenitsky and Giovanni Pagnotta Client: Altec Lansing (bottom) 'MNA Gaming Satellite' Design Firm: Macey Noyes Associates Creative Director: Tod Dawson Designers: Lenny Dichiara, Victor Ivenitsky and Giovanni Pagnotta Client: Altec Lansing Products 216,217

(top) '5.1 Gaming Speakers Group' Design Firm: Macey Noyes Associates Creative Director: Tod Dawson Designers: Lenny Dichiara, Victor

(this spread) 'Mould (Chair)' Design Firm: Aersus Art Directors: Kazutoshi Amano and Shinichi Sasaki Designers: Kazutoshi Amano and Shinichi Sasaki Client: Aersus

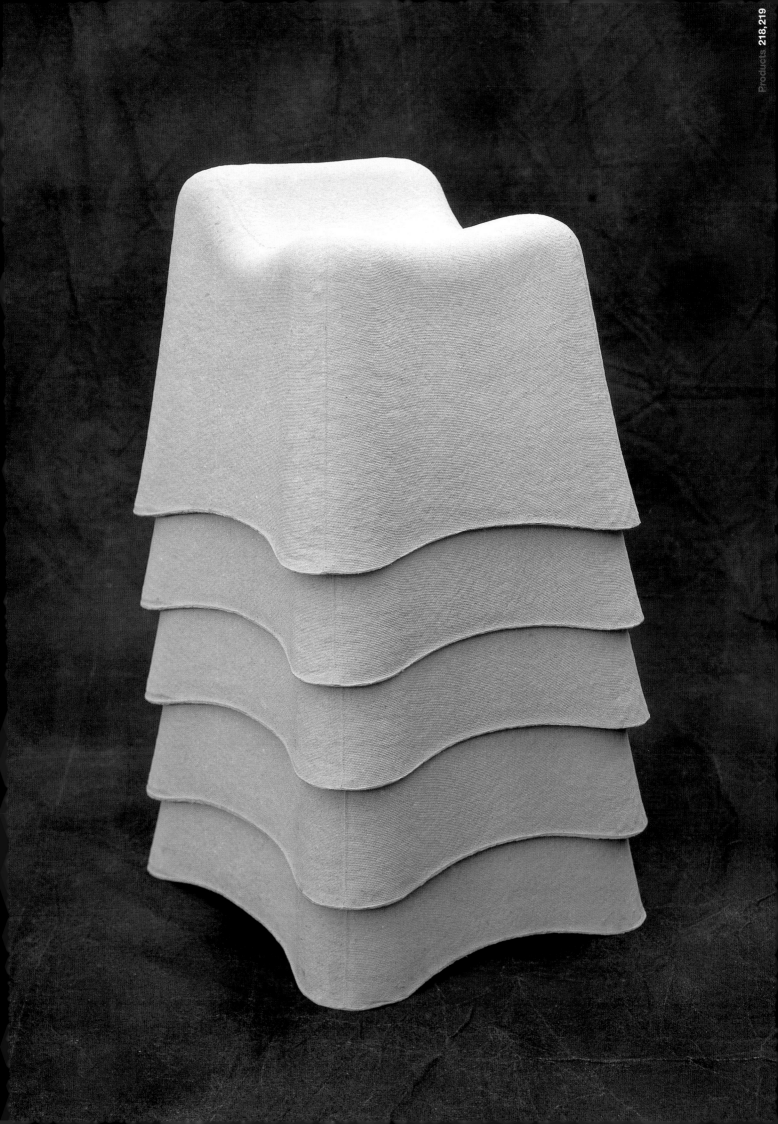

Applied Typography 11 Design Firm: Shinnoske, Inc. Art Director: Shinnoske Sugisaki Designer: Shinnoske Sugisaki Client: Japan Typography Association   Promotions 220,221

Design Firm: Larsen Design & Interactive Creative Director: Richelle J. Huff Designers: Anna Giacomini; Liina Koukkari and Wendy Ruyle Copywriters: Rick Emerson and Ann Bauleke Client: American Express Financial Advisors

'Prosciutto di Parma' Design Firm: BBI Studio, Inc. Art Director: Zempaku Suzuki Designers: Zempaku Suzuki and Aki Hirai Photographer: Tamotsu Ikeda Copywriter: Asako Yamazaki Client: Italian Trade Commission

(top) 'Branding Iron' Design Firm: Kilmer & Kilmer Creative Director: Richard Kilmer Designers: Randall Marshall and Randall Marshall Client: Kilmer & Kilmer (bottom) Design Firm: Kilmer & Kilmer Creative Director: Richard Kilmer Art Director: Richard Kilmer Designers: Randall Marshall and Eldin Cooper Client: Kilmer & Kilmer

Buckle,' 'Barbwire' and 'Snake' Design Firm: Bailey Lauerman Creative Director: Marty Amsler Art Director: Marty Amsler Photographer: David Radler Copywriters: John Vogel and Nick Main Client: Nebraska Film Office

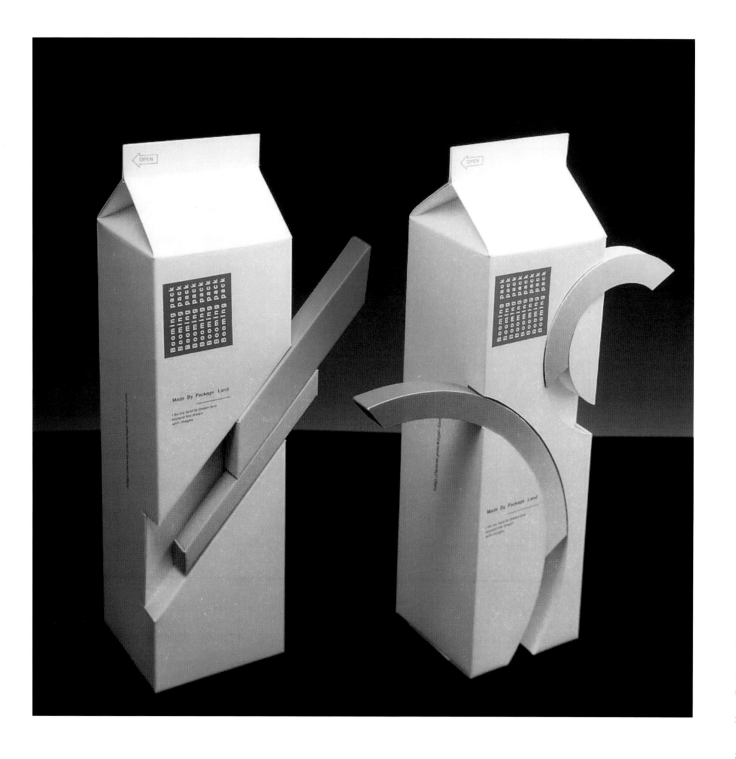

Design Firm: Package Land Co. Ltd. Creative Director: Yasuo Tanaka Art Director: Yasuo Tanaka Designer: Yasuo Tanaka Photographer: Yasuo Tanaka Client: Package Land Co. Ltd.　　Promotions 228, 229

Terry Heffernan—known in the worlds of advertising and design for his exquisite large-format still lifes— has quietly pursued his passion of photographing iconic images that capture the soul of America. All of the portraits shown were shot on location using an 8x10 camera with available light.

"An icon is the visual shorthand of a culture."

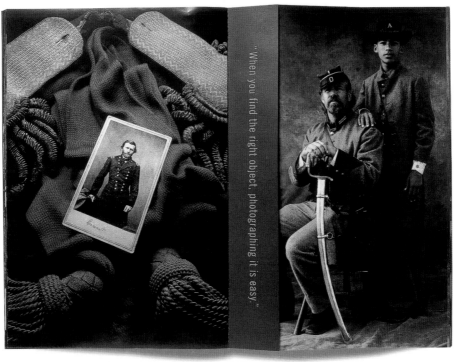

"When you find the right object, photographing it is easy."

Design Firm: Pentagram Design, Inc. Art Director: Kit Hinrichs Designer: David Asari Photographer: Terry Heffernan Copywriter: Delphine Hirasuna Client: Terry Heffernan

Portfolio No. 036

Since the beginning of consumerism, the humble tin has been one of the most enduring forms of product design.

A simple, robust method of preserving food, the tin became a brilliant way of advertising and presenting goods and, thanks to Warhol's soup cans, a consumer icon in itself.

We saw a parallel between the tin and our own ambitions; applying simple and robust design solutions to our work, thereby brilliantly influencing consumer culture ourselves.

British Airways

Designing a new interior for Concorde is not just about new seats and a new bathroom, but the creation of a unique experience—combining the expectation and the emotion of flying in the world's only commercial supersonic jet.

Concorde remains to many the most elegant aircraft in the skies. Factory had to ensure that this elegance was reflected in the new interior to enhance the experience of travelling on this unique aircraft. To move beyond current aircraft seating and bring fresh thought to the seat, Factory looked outside the traditional aircraft industry for both the construction and the nature of the design.

Today any business class seat is larger, with more features than seats on Concorde, so Factory's design owes more to a blend of Formula One technology and an executive boardroom chair than to traditional aircraft seating. These leather seats, with aluminium speedmarque arms, moving head and foot rests are also more comfortable. Using composite materials like carbon fibre, Factory designed a cradle seat as a single monocoque moulding which avoids making separate parts, saving the cost and weight of fixings to join them—each part performing a structural or functional task rather than simply providing decoration.

The toilet was re-named the Bathroom and designed to reflect the calm refinement you would expect in the washroom of a good hotel or restaurant. White flannel towels, not paper tissues and taps from the best in the domestic market, not typical airline fittings, combine with other details to give the Bathroom a contemporary appeal. Factory even found more room by moving storage cabinets into unused cabin space. Simplicity of detail and careful use of light and mirrors create a more elegant bathroom which appears and feels larger.

Breaking the speed of sound is a special moment, but there is no sign of this happening other than a bulkhead machmeter display. Many devices were considered to celebrate this moment before settling on a discrete yet visible wave of blue light that pulses from the front to the rear of Concorde in a second, stays lit for a few seconds, then disappears.

A simple yet quietly dramatic display which rewards any passengers watching for 'change' without disturbing regular passengers trying to work or rest. Just one example of Factory's ambition to embrace the theatre of supersonic travel.

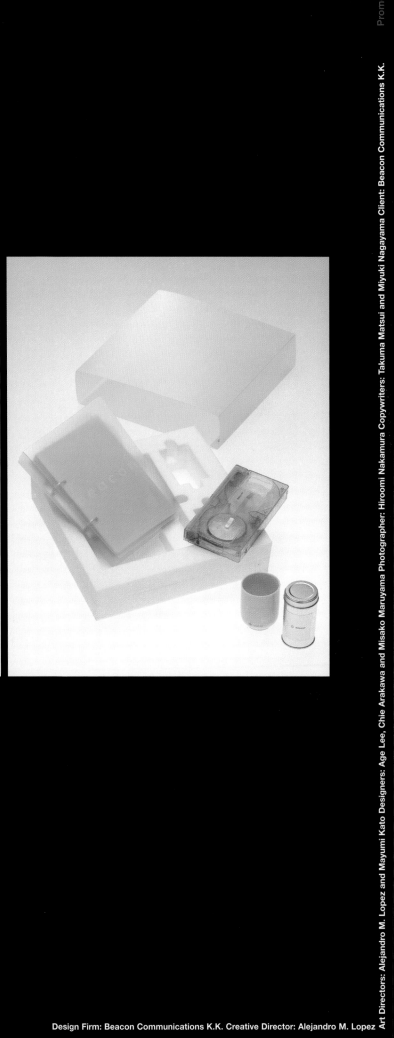

Art Directors: Alejandro M. Lopez and Mayumi Kato Designers: Age Lee, Chie Arakawa and Misako Maruyama Photographer: Hiroomi Nakamura Copywriters: Takuma Matsui and Miyuki Nagayama Client: Beacon Communications K.K.

Design Firm: Beacon Communications K.K. Creative Director: Alejandro M. Lopez

Design Firm: Beacon Communications K.K. Creative Director: Alejandro M. Lopez Art Director: Mayumi Kato Designers: Chie Arakawa, Misako Maruyama and Akiko Tanaka Client: Beacon Communications K.K.

Design Firm: Sandstrom Design Creative Director: Steve Sandstrom Art Director: Steve Sandstrom Designer: Steve Sandstrom Production Designer: Andrew Randall Client: Tazo

'AP' Design Firm: Akio Okumura Art Director: Akio Okumura Designer: Sae Nagaoka Client: Access Publishing

human intellect

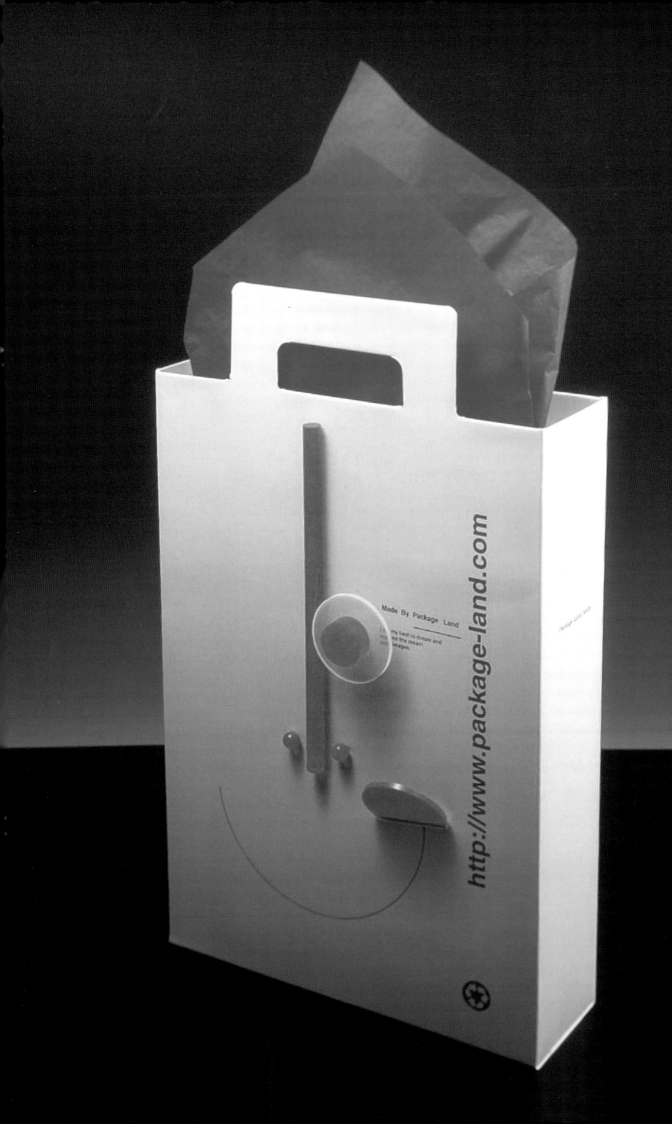

Made By Package Land

http://www.package-land.com

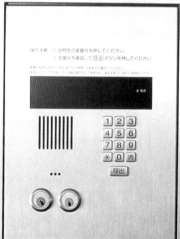

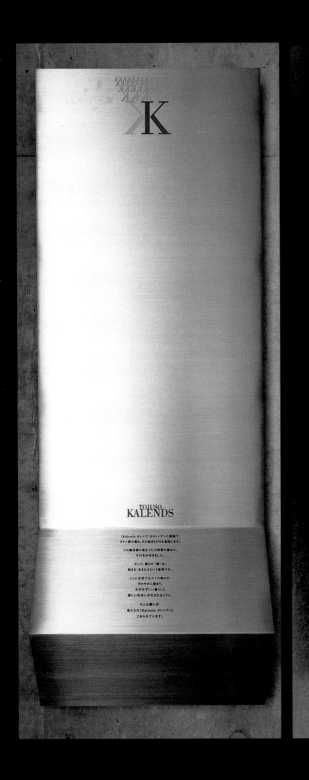

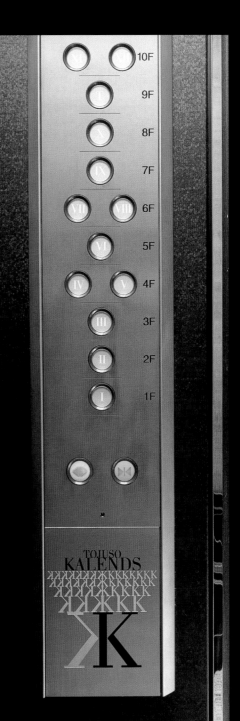

(this spread) Design Firm: Shinnoske Inc. Creative Director: Osamu Nakasuji Art Director: Shinnoske Sugisaki Designers: Shinnoske Sugisaki and Chiaki Okuno Client: Tojuso Kalends Cooperative

(top) 'Porto 2001, Capital Europeia da Cultura' Design Firm: João Machado Design, Lda. Creative Director: João Machado Art Director: João Machado Designer: João Machado Illustrator: João Machado Client: CTT (bottom) 'Água Riqueza Natural' Design Firm: João

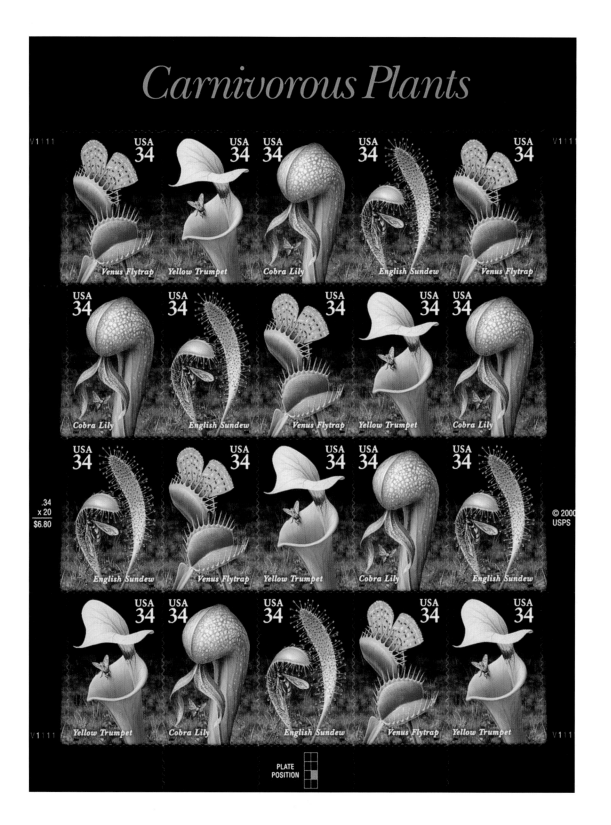

If your body is perfekt,
but your brain is not,
go and invest in it:
Cut out this

VOUCHER

and bring it with the
receipt to smart
INTERCELL and you'll
get

ats **1000,**

€72,673

© Original English by Cosima+Cordula

DIALECTICAL MATERIAL IN ACTION.

AIRSPACE.

A LIE MAY MEAN A VICTORY TODAY, BUT IT MEANS A DEFEAT TOMORROW.

WALL

OF

NOISE

BE A GOOD

CITIZEN

BACK DIE

AND N.E NY

OR

SC FORTH

DON'T PEE ON ME

A DANGEROUS
BLEND OF
POETRY
AND
PROPAGANDA

JOIN

A DANGEROUS
BLEND OF
GRAPHIC SOLUTIONS
FOR AN AMENABLE
WORLD

USOFA

URAMERICAN
SERIF · THICK OUTLINE · CLASSIC · OUTLINE · CAPS

(this spread) 'My Proletariat Life' Design Firm: Slow-motion Art Director: Jeff Miller Designer: Jeff Miller Client: Type-M

A	B	C	D	E	F	G	H	I	K	L	M	N	O	P	Q	R	S	T	U
V	W	X	Y	Z	J	Á	Í	Ó	Ú	Ä	Ö	Ő	Ü	Ű					
1	2	3	4	5	6	7	8	9	0	–	)	(	[	el	@	®	,	"	*
#	œ				j	á	é	í	ó	ú	ö	ő	ü	ű	..	∗	⁂	⁂	
•	\$				s		t	u	r		w	x		z					
+	%									v			y	–					
∴	÷			k	h		m		i		n		o		q				
∨	/	1 pont		l											p				
ê	¢	1.5 pont		a		e		d		2 cicero	3 cicero		Negyed						
à	ä	2 pont		b							f		g		4 cicero				

Harmad · Negyzet · Félnégyzet

CreativeDirectorsArtDirectorsDesigners

CreativeDirectorsArtDirectorsDesigners

PhotographersIllustrators

Copywriters

Design Firms

Clients

Directory of Design Firms

3.Kusak
Kügükbebek Cad. 2/6
Istanbul, Turkey 80810
Tel: 90 21 2257 2815
Fax: 90 21 2263 5281
www.3kusak.com

344 Design, LLC
101 N Grand Ave
Pasadena, CA 91103
Tel: 1 626 796 5148
www.344design.com

Aersus
Fuji Building 3F, 1-11-6 Ebisu,
Shibuya-ku
Tokyo, Japan 150-0013
Tel: 81 3 5795 1588
Fax: 81 3 5795 1589

Agency Eleven
10,000 Highway 55
Minneapolis, MN 55441
Tel: 1 763 595 5810
Fax: 1 763 595 5815
www.agencyeleven.com

Akio Okumura
Commemorative Association for the
Japan World Exposition 1F 1-1 Senri
Banpaku-Koen, Suite A
Osaka, Japan 565-0826
Tel: 81 6 4864 6380
Fax: 81 6 4864 6570
www.okumura-akio.com

Alessandri Design
Rufgasse 3, Fabrik Im Hof
Vienna, Austria 1090
Tel: 43 1 310 44 01
Fax: 43 1 310 44 01 20

Ando Studio
541 Commerce Street 5
Franklin Lakes, NJ 07417
Tel: 1 201 405 0301
Fax: 1 201 405 0717

Artworks
Csmete U.3
Budapest, Hungary 1036
Tel: 36 1 437 1358
Fax: 36 1 437 1399
www.artworks.co.hu

Atelier Works
5 Charlton Kings Road
London, United Kingdom NE52SB
Tel: 44 20 7284 2215
Fax: 44 20 7284 2242
www.atelierworks.co.uk

[b] studios
1600 Park Circle Suite 914
Columbia, SC 29201
Tel: 1 803 781 8091
Fax: 1 803 781 3269

Bad Studio
1123 Zonolite Road Suite 18
Atlanta, GA 30306
Tel: 1 404 881 1977
Fax: 1 404 881 1966
www.badgraphics.com

Bailey Lauerman
900 Wells Fargo Center
Lincoln, NE 68508
Tel: 1 402 475 2800
Fax: 1 402 475 5115
www.baileylauerman.com

BBI Studio, Inc.
Oxson 3rd Floor, 1-2-13, Shintomi,
Chuoku
Tokyo, Japan 104-0041
Tel: 81 3 3552 6960
Fax: 81 3 3552 6950

Beacon Communications K.K.
2-17-22 Akasaka, Minato-Ku
Tokyo, Japan 107-8535
Tel: 813 5563 8390
Fax: 813 3584 2845
www.beaconcom.co.jp

BIG Werbeagentur oHG
Augustastrasse 30
Düsseldorf, Germany 40477
Tel: 49 211 440389940
Fax: 49 211 44038979
www.big.ag

Bradford Lawton Design Group, Inc.
1020 Townsend
San Antonio, TX 78209
Tel: 1 210 832 0555
Fax: 1 210 832 0001

www.bradfordlawton.com

CGI Brandsense
16 Shorts Gardens
London, United Kingdom W45PY
Tel: 44 20 7379 1122
Fax: 44 20 7379 3883
www.grundynorthedge.com

Chen Design Associates
589 Howard Street
San Francisco, CA 94105
Tel: 1 415 896 5338
Fax: 1 415 896 5339
www.chendesign.com

Chirstina Ullman Design
36395 Greenbrick Road
Graysville, OH 45734
Tel: 1 740 934 9321

David Lancashire Design
17 William Street
Richmond, Victoria
Australia 3121
Tel: 03 9421 4509
Fax: 03 9421 4569
www.lancashire.com.au

DDB Brand Sellers
Tehaankatu 29 A
Helsinki, Finland 00150
Tel: 3589 584 584
Fax: 3589 626 833
www.bsddb.fi

Design Bridge Ltd.
18 Clerkenwell Close
London, United Kingdom
EC1ROQN
Tel: 44 20 7418 1108
Fax: 44 20 7814 9024
www.designbridge.co.uk

Design Guys
119 North 4th Street 400
Minneapolis, MN 55401
Tel: 1 612 338 4462
Fax: 1 612 338 1875
www.designguys.com

Design Hoch Drei
Hallstrasse 25A

Stuttgart, Germany 70376
Tel: 49 711 55037730
Fax: 49 711 55037755
www.design-hoch-drei.de

Design M:W
149 Wooster Street
New York, NY 10012
Tel: 1 212 982 7621
Fax: 1 212 982 7630
www.designmw.com

DNA Design Ltd.
L2, 262 Thorndon Quay
Wellington, New Zealand
Tel: 614 499 0828
Fax: 614 499 0888
www.dna.co.nz

Duffy Minneapolis
50 South 6th Street
Minneapolis, MN 55402
Tel: 1 612 758 2512
Fax: 1 612 758 2334
www.duffy.com

E-Fact Ltd.
159-173 St. John Street
London, United Kingdom EC1V4R5
Tel: 44 207 8804733
Fax: 44 207 8804799
www.e-fact.com

Eden Design Communication
Prinsengracht 8G
Amsterdam, The Netherlands 1018 VR
Tel: 31 20 712 3000
Fax: 31 20 712 3123
www.edendesign.nl

El Comercio
Jr. Miro Quesada 300
Lima, Peru 01
Tel: 511 4264676

Fax: 511 4264676 x3659
www.comercio.com.pe

Emery Vincent Design, Sydney
Level 1, 15 Foster Street
Surry Hills, New South Wales
Australia 2010
Tel: 61 2 9280 4233

Fax: 61 2 9280 4266
www.emeryvincentdesign.com

Epigram
75 Sophia Road
Singapore, 228156
Tel: 65 292 4456
Fax: 65 292 4414

Equus Design Consultants P/L
8B Murray Terrace
Singapore 079522
Tel: 65 323 2996
Fax: 65 323 2991
www.equus-design.com

Esther Noyons
Leimuidenstraat 2
Amsterdam, Holland 1059EH
Tel: 31 20 669020252
Fax: 31 20 6690227

Fossil
2280 North Greenville Avenue
Richardson, TX 75082
Tel: 1 972 699 2285
Fax: 1 972 699 2071
www.fossil.com

Fountainhead Design
P.O. Box 721, Green Point
Cape Town, South Africa 8051
Tel: 2721 4194822
Fax: 2721 4195700
www.fountainhead.co.sa

Gail Anderson
81 Bedford Street Apt. 3E
New York, NY 10014
Tel: 1 212 645 2847

Giraffe Werbeagentur GmbH
Leipziger Strasse 187
Frankfurt, Germany 15232
Tel: 49 335 50 46 46
Fax: 49 335 50 46 45
www.giraffe.de

Gollings & Pidgeon
147 Chapel Street, St. Kilda
Melbourne, Australia 3182
Tel: 61 3 9537 0733
Fax: 61 3 9537 0187
www.gollingspidgeon.com

Gottschalk & Ash International
11 Bishop Street
Toronto, Ontario
Canada M5R 1N3
Tel: 1 416 963 9717
Fax: 1 416 963 9351

Graphica Design & Communications
4501 Lyons Road
Miamisburg, OH 45342
Tel: 1 937 866 4013
Fax: 1 937 866 5581
www.graphicadesign.com

Haefelinger Wagner Design
Erhardtstrasse
Muenchen, Germany D80649
Tel: 49 89 202575 0
Fax: 49 89 2023 9696
www.hwdesign.de

Happy Forsman & Bodenfors
Kungsgatan 51
Gothenburg, Sweden
Tel: 46 3133 96200
Fax: 46 3133 96201
www.happy.fb.se

Hornall Anderson Design Works
1008 Western Avenue, Suite 600
Seattle, WA 98104
Tel: 1 206 467 5800
Fax: 1 206 467 6411
www.hadw.com

i.design
6030 Morningside Avenue
Dallas, TX 75206
Tel: 1 214 826 6228
Fax: 1 214 826 6855
www.ingramdesign.com

IA Collaborative
215 West Institute Place
Chicago, IL 60610
Tel: 1 312 337 2126
Fax: 1 312 337 2367
www.iacollaborative.com

Ibbison Design Associates (IDA)
56A South Molton Street
London, United Kingdom W1K5SH
Tel: 44 20 7499 2333
Fax: 44 20 7499 2442

IE Design, Los Angeles
1600 Rosencrans Avenue
Manhattan Beach, CA
Tel: 1 310 727 3500
Fax: 1 310 727 3515
www.iedesign.net

Jager di Paola Kemp
47 Maple Street
Burlington, VT 05401
Tel: 1 802 864 5884
Fax: 1 802 864 8039
www.jdk.com

João Machado Design, Lda.
Rua Padre Xavier Coutinho, 125
Porto, Portugal 4150-751
Tel: 35 1226 1037 72 78
Fax: 35 1226 1037 73
www.joaomachado.com

Karacters Design Group
1600-777 Hornby Street
Vancouver, British Columbia
Canada V6Z2T3
Tel: 604 640 4327
Fax: 604 608 4452
www.karacters.com

Kellum McClain Inc.
151 First Avenue PH-1
New York, NY 10003
Tel: 1 212 979 2661
Fax: 1 212 260 3525

Kennard Design
20 Park Plaza #720
Boston, MA 02116
Tel: 1 617 338 8667
Fax: 1 617 426 8559
www.kennarddesign.com

Kilmer & Kilmer
125 Truman NE, Suite 200
Albuquerque, NM 87108
Tel: 1 505 260 1175
Fax: 1 505 260 1155
www.kilmer2.com

Kokokumaru Inc.
509 Unihigashiumeda 7-2, Mi-
namiogimachi Kitaku

Osaka, Japan
Larsen Design & Interactive
7101 York Avenue South
Minneapolis, MN 55435
Tel: 1 952 835 2271
Fax: 1 952 835 3368
www.larsen.com

Laughlin/Constable - Griffin Design
207 East Michigan Street
Milwaukee, WI 53202
Tel: 1 414 272 2400
Fax: 1 414 298 1133
www.laughlin.com

Lewis Moberly
33 Gresse Street
London, United Kingdom W1T
1QU
Tel: 44 20 7580 9252
Fax: 44 20 7255 1671
www.lewismoberly.com

Louey/Rubino Design Group
2525 Main Street, Suite 204
Santa Monica, CA 90405
Tel: 1 310 396 7724
Fax: 1 310 396 1686
www.loueyrubino.com

Macey Noyes Associates
232 Danbury Road
Wilton, CT 06897
Tel: 1 203 762 9002
Fax: 1 203 762 2679
www.maceynoyes.com

Malcolm Waddell Assoicates
6 Yule Avenue
Toronto, Ontario
Canada M6S1E8
Tel: 1 416 761 1737
Fax: 1 416 761 9684

Mauk Design
39 Stillman Street
San Francisco, CA 94107
Tel: 1 415 243 9277
Fax: 1 415 243 9278
www.maukdesign.com

Michael Schwab Studio
108 Tamalpais Avenue
San Anselmo, CA 94960
Tel: 1 415 257 5792
Fax: 1 415 257 5793
www.michaelschwab.com

Mires
2345 Kettner Boulevard
San Diego, CA 92101
Tel: 1 619 234 6631
Fax: 1 619 234 1807
www.miresbrands.com

Mirko Ilic Corp.
207 East 32nd Street
New York, NY 10016
Tel: 1 212 481 9737
Fax: 1 212 481 7088

Moses Media
584 Broadway, #607
New York City, NY 10012
Tel: 1 212 625 0331
www.mosesmedia.com

Mucca Design
315 Church St 4th Fl
New York, NY 10013
Tel: 1 212 965 9821
Fax: 1 212 965 8524
www.muccadesign.com

NDW Communications
100 Tournament Dr. Suite 230
Horsham, PA 19044
Tel: 1 215 957 9871
Fax: 1 215 957 9872
www.ndwc.com

Newton.Ehb
13-15 Circus Lane
Edinburgh, United Kingdom
EH36SU
Tel: 44 131 220 4141
Fax: 44 131 220 4004
www.newtonehb.com

North Castle Design
15 Blank Street
Stamford, CT 06901
Tel: 1 203 358 2136
Fax: 1 203 353 8699
www.northcastledesign.com

Osamu Misawa Design Room

#202 3-13-20 Sendagaya, Shibuya-
Ku
Tokyo, Japan 151 0051
Tel: 81 3 5772 2765
Fax: 81 3 5772 2785
www.omdr.co.jp

p11creative
20331 Irvine Avenue, #E-5
Santa Ana Heights, CA 92707
Tel: 1 714 641 2090
Fax: 1 714 641 2894
www.p11.com

Package Land Co. Ltd.
201 Tezukayama Tower Plaza 1-3-2
Tezukayama Naka
Sumiyoshi-Ku Osaka, Japan 5580053
Tel: 06 6675 0138
Fax: 06 6675 6466
www.package-land.com

Pentagram Design, Austin
1508 West Fifth Street
Austin, TX 78703
Tel: 1 512 476 3076
Fax: 1 512 476 3076
www.pentagram.com

Pentagram Design Inc.
387 Tehama
San Francisco, CA 94103
Tel: 1 415 896 0499
Fax: 1 415 896 0555
www.pentagram.com

Pentagram Design Ltd.
11 Needham Road
London, United Kingdom W112RP
Tel: 44 20 7229 3477
Fax: 44 20 7727 9932
www.pentagram.co.uk

Peterson & Company
2200 North Lamar, Suite 310
Dallas, TX 75202
Tel: 1 214 954 0522
Fax: 1 214 954 1161
www.peterson.com

Planet Propaganda
605 Williamson Street
Madison, WI 53703
Tel: 1 608 256 0000
Fax: 1 608 256 1975
www.planetpropaganda.com

Popglory
8460 Cole Crest Drive
Los Angeles, CA 90046
Tel: 1 323 656 5502
Fax: 1 323 656 5320
www.popglory.com

RBMM
7007 Twin Hills
Dallas, TX 75231
Tel: 1 214 987 6500
Fax: 1 214 987 3662
www.rbmm.com

Red Canoe
347 Clear Creek Trail
Deer Lodge, TN 37726
Tel: 1 423 965 2223
Fax: 1 423 965 1005
www.redcanoe.com

Rolling Stone
1290 Avenue of the Americas
New York, NY 10104
Tel: 1 212 484 1658
Fax: 1 212 484 1664
www.rollingstone.com

Rose-Innes Associates
184 Leighton Road
London, United Kingdom NW52RE
Tel: 44 20 7482 4004
Fax: 44 20 7482 2536

Sagmeister, Inc.
222 West 14th Street
New York, NY 10011
Tel: 1 212 647 1789
Fax: 1 212 647 1788

Sandstrom Design
808 Southwest Third Avenue, #610
Portland, OR 97204
Tel: 1 503 248 9466
Fax: 1 503 227 5035
www.sandstromdesign.com

Sasaki Assoicates
64 Pleasant Street
Watertown, MA 02472
Tel: 1 617 926 3300

Fax: 1 617 924 2748
jdbarry@sasaki.com

Savas Cekic Design Studio
Havyar Sk. 27/3 Cihangir
Istanbul, Turkey 80060
Tel: 90 212 249 6918
Fax: 90 212 245 5009
www.savascekic.com

Sayles Graphic Design
3701 Beaver Avenue
Des Moines, IA 50310
Tel: 1 515 279 2922
Fax: 1 515 279 0212
www.saylesdesign.com

Scheufele Kommunikations-Agentur
Gr. Friedberger Strasse 13
Frankfurt, Germany 60313
Tel: 49 69 1387100
Fax: 49 69 1387126
info@scheufele-nc.de

Scooter Design
14 Imperial Terrace
Wellington, New Zealand 5953
Tel: 64 4 387 3661

Shinnoske, Inc.
602 Tsurigane-cho, Chuo-ku
Osaka-shi, Osaka Japan 540 0035
Tel: 81 6 6943 9077
Fax: 81 6 6943 9078
www.shinn.co.jp

Sibley Peteet Design
2905 San Gabriel Suite 300
Austin, TX 78705
Tel: 1 512 473 2333
Fax: 1 512 743 2431

Slow-motion
4973 1/2 Franklin Avenue
Los Angeles, CA 90027
Tel: 1 323 644 0042

Sony Music
550 Madison Avenue
New York, NY 10022
Tel: 1 212 833 7117
Fax: 1 212 833 4388
www.sonymusic.com

Sparc, Inc.
1735 North Paulina #502
Chicago, IL 60622
Tel: 1 773 772 1600
Fax: 1 773 772 3800

Strichpunkt GmbH
Schönleinstrasse 8a
Stuttgart, Germany 70184
Tel: 49 711 620327 0
Fax: 49 711 620327 10
www.strichpunkt-design.de

Sullivan Perkins
2811 McKinney Avenue, Suite 320
Dallas, TX 75204
Tel: 1 214 922 9080
Fax: 1 214 922 0044
www.sullivanperkins.com

T. G. Madison Advertising
3340 Peachtree Road Suite 2850
Atlanta, GA 30326
Tel: 1 404 262 2623
Fax: 1 404 237 2811
www.tgmadison.com

Taku Satoh Design Office Inc.
Ginsho Building 4F, 1-14-11 Ginza,
Chuoku
Tokyo, Japan
Tel: 81 3 3538 2501
Fax: 81 3 21 3538 2054
www.tsdo.co.jp

Taxi
495 Wellington Street West
Toronto, Ontario
Canada M5VIE9
Tel: 1 416 979 4402
Fax: 1 416 979 7626
www.taxi.ca

TBWA/PHS
Tehtaankatu 1A
Helsinki, Finland FIN00140
Tel: 358 9 171 711
Fax: 358 9 171 811
www.phs.fi

Templin Brink Design
720 Tehama Street
San Francisco, CA 94103

Tel: 1 415 255 9295
Fax: 1 415 255 9296
cblacker@tdb-sf.com

Th
422-3 Main Street
Franklin, TN 37064
Tel: 1 615 790 2777
Fax: 1 615 790 2377
www.thwastaken.com

The Designory, Inc.
211 East Ocean Boulevard, Suite 100
Long Beach 90803
Tel: 1 562 624 0346
Fax: 1 562 432 4035
www.designory.com

The McCulley Group
415 South Cedros Avenue Studio 240
Solana Beach, CA 92075
Tel: 1 858 259 5222
Fax: 1 858 259 1877
www.mcculleygroup.com

There Media
410 West 14th Street
New York, NY 10014
Tel: 1 212 366 4140
www.there.com

Thom & Dave Marketing Design
28 West State Street
Media, PA 19063
Tel: 1 610 566 0566
Fax: 1 610 892 0151
www.thomdave.com

Vanderbyl Design
171 Second Street
San Francisco, CAUnited States
94105
Tel: 1 415 543 8447
Fax: 1 415 543 9058
www.vanderbyl.com

Vinte Zero Um
Rua Humaitá 85/201
Rio De Janeiro, Brasil 22261 000
Tel: 55 21 2527 9268
Fax: 55 21 2527 9268
www.vintezeroum.com

Vitro Robertson
1111 6th Avenue
San Diego, CA 92101
Tel: 1 619 234 0408
Fax: 1 619 234 0415
www.vitrorobertson.com

VSA Partners Inc.
1347 S. State Street
Chicago, IL 60605
Tel: 1 312 427 6413
Fax: 1 312 427 3246

Wallace Church, Inc.
330 East 48th Street
New York, NY 10017
Tel: 1 212 755 2903
Fax: 1 212 355 6872
www.wallacechurch.com

Weigertpirouzwolf
Waterloohain 5
Hamburg, Germany 22769
Tel: 49 1 40 43239 0
Fax: 49 1 40 43239 222
www.weigertpirouzwolf.de

Williams Murrary Hamm
Heals Building, Alfred Mews
London, England WIP97B
Tel: 44 20 7255 3232
Fax: 44 20 7636 4593
www.creatingdifference.com

Wittman Idea Network
968 Farmington Avenue
West Hartford, CT 06107
Tel: 1 860 232 7170
Fax: 1 860 232 7174
www.wittmanideas.com

Wren & Rowe Ltd.
4 Denbigh Mews
London, United Kingdom SWI2HQ
Tel: 44 20 7828 5333
Fax: 44 20 7828 5444
www.wrenrowe.co.uk

zefrank.com
176 Amity Street Apartment 3R
Brooklyn, NY 11201
Tel: 1 718 596 4907
www.zefrank.com